The Duke

Praise for *The Duke*

"Scott Kerman humanizes Michael Dukakis -- presidential candidate, three-term Massachusetts governor, community role model, bane of litterers -- with humor and insight that reveal a multi-layered man of deep civic passions who's thoughtful, irreverent, and refreshingly comfortable in his own skin. A delight to read."

~ Brian MacQuarrie, Boston Globe

"Humorist Scott Kerman shows us that decades after being out of office one of America's best known political leaders still has so much to say by opening his heart – and his mouth."

~ Stephen Kurkjian, Three-time Pulitzer- prize winner for Boston Globe

"The Duke is both hilarious and touching as Humorist Scott Kerman recounts his long relationship with former Massachusetts Gov. Mike Dukakis, a simply lovable character. If you are looking for humor, nostalgia and a just-plain-fun read, you've got to pick this book up."

~ Executive Editor, Tracey Rauh, The Eagle-Tribune

Also by Scott J. Kerman

All Sold Out!

No Ticket? No Problem!

Millennials!@#!

World According to Scott!

World According to Scott! The Sequel

World According to Scott! The Third book

For information about permission to reproduce
selections from the book or to interview the author,
please write to curzonmillpublishing@gmail.com

ISBN: 979-8-2829-8398-2 (Paperback)

Book cover design by Scott J. Kerman
All photos by Scott J. Kerman and copyrighted ©sjk2025

Printed in the United States.
DOC 10 9 8 7 6 5 4 3 2 1

The Duke

Weekly Conversations with the
Last Honest Politician

A Political Giant and a comedian
walk into a kitchen…

Scott J. Kerman

Curzon Mill Publishing
Brookline, MA
2025

The book is dedicated to
Governor Michael S. Dukakis
and his wife Kitty Dukakis.

Contents

Acknowledgments

To my wonderful wife, Adrienne Kerman, thank you for your constant encouragement and never-ending support for this book and in everything I do. I am forever grateful to travel these roads with you.

My sincerest gratitude to the following for their assistance and contribution to this book:

The Dukakis Family
Leila Joy Rosenthal for her editorial assistance; and
Dave Ives for his fact-checking and critical review.

The Duke

Make That Two Scoops

I first met Governor Michael Dukakis on August 26, 1977 at the age of 11. My parents had an ice cream smorgasbord fundraiser for his re-election campaign in our back yard in my hometown of Methuen, Mass.

I was a husky kid. That's what polite, older folks and the Sears Boys' Department called chubby boys back then. Smart ass adults and crappy kids called you fat. I was still growing into my body and mind. It makes you hungry. I was enjoying my second ice cream cone on that hot summer day, working hard to defend my husky title, when out of nowhere (which is how everyone appears when entering a backyard) came the current governor of the Commonwealth of Massachusetts, Michael Dukakis. He was walking on the very same grass where my friends and I played baseball. He was a distinguished man decked out in a dress shirt and tie with no suit coat. He looked like a school principal or a city councilman. His pace and stride screamed that of a man with places to go and people to see.

The first thing I thought when I saw him was how my mother had yelled at me to wear a dress shirt and to find a "nice clip-on tie." (Do nice clip-on ties exist?) I'm glad I didn't wear one. I would've looked like the Governor. No 11-year-old kid wanted to look like any adult. We didn't even talk to adults we weren't related to or who weren't our teachers. If I was in a room with my friends' parents, I shit my husky pants.

My father had told my mother, "Let Scotty wear what he's comfortable in." So I wore a blue t-shirt, nylon gym shorts, striped, calf-length athletic socks and my trusty Keds. My father always had my back. He was sporting a nice blue summer suit and looked snappy enough to rep all the Kerman boys that day.

The Governor worked our backyard like the seasoned politician he was, shaking the hands of attendees, bobbing and weaving from one group to the next and spending a little extra time with my parents, the host and hostess. He was the Sugar Ray Leonard of the social circuit, looking you straight in the eye so you'd know you had his full attention and that he's within reach. You'd lean in to say a second sentence following your, "It's nice to meet you, Governor," and—Bang!—he's already with the next person.

I remember once when I was nine years old at a cook-out and stuck in conversation with my boorish uncle as he droned on about the differences between grass and weeds. By the time I was set free, all the sugar cookies were gone. It still pains me to this day. Also, there is no difference. You smoke both.

Our family got together and took a group photo with the Governor. The Governor was in the middle, and I was at the far right. As a middle child you learn young that you're expendable. In every family vacation photo, I was placed at the end so that if I died, they could easily cut me out of the photo and still ensure that fun family memory remained preserved.

After the photo op, I stayed back and watched the maestro at work. The Governor would not have lost out on any cookies. I let all the grown-ups get their brief touches while waiting for the Governor to make it to the ice cream table, clearly my area of comfort. He eventually made it to the table where I was standing with the server, my sister, Leslie. "Hey, Sis, give the Governor an extra scoop of coffee ice cream on me," I said. She nervously laughed and gave me a look like she wanted to kick me in the nuts.

The Governor and I shook hands and started talking about the Red Sox. There was no soiling of the shorts here, despite him being the most famous person I had ever met. Instantly, he seemed like an uncle to me. The Red Sox was the only subject I could talk to my father about on an equal level. Another comfort zone.

In 1977, the Red Sox had a powerhouse offensive team that consisted of Rice, Lynn, Yaz, Boomer, Fisk, and Evans. They were superheroes to an eleven-year-old. This team was going to win the World Series title that the 1975 team had come just one game shy of claiming. The painful fifty-nine-year streak of no World Series victories would finally end for Sox fans. I can die in peace! Actually, that wasn't even a rallying cry. It would take the devastating 1986 World Series loss to really let loose the epic whining of the *Curse of the Bambino*. The 1977 team went on to win 97 games but faded at the end and finished second place to the New York Yankees. And my hatred of the Yanks grew. Losing to the pinstripes always felt different.

The Governor had already known both victory and defeat in his political life. He'd served four terms in the Massachusetts House of Representatives between 1962 and 1970. In 1966, Dukakis lost the race to be the attorney general of Massachusetts. In 1970, he was the Democratic nominee for lieutenant governor on a ticket led by Boston Mayor Kevin White—a ticket that eventually lost the 1970 gubernatorial election. He went on to win the race for governor in 1974, defeating the incumbent Republican, Francis Sargent.

He asked me who my favorite player was and I said Fred Lynn. Then, as I started to begin ripping into the manager Don Zimmer— Kapow!—the Governor was gone to finish shaking hands and move on to a ham and bean supper in Lawrence. Or something like that. I was left with a melted cup of strawberry ice cream. In retrospect, I shouldn't have gone negative. There was no room for negativity at an ice cream smorgasbord or a presidential campaign. Or at least that's what I would learn later. I shadowed him enough to watch him jump in his car as he wrapped up the last of his coffee ice cream cone.

Who knew 11 years from then, Governor Dukakis would be on the precipice of being the most powerful person in the world? And I would be wearing normal-sized pants.

The Grandstanders

I sit in the studio waiting to begin our talk show's annual episode with former Governor Dukakis, or as we affectionately call him, the Duke. The show was set to start at 7:00 pm. It's now 7:15 and he has not yet arrived.

I host a weekly Boston sports TV show and podcast called *The Grandstanders Live*, which is taped in Brookline, Mass, where both Dukakis and I live. My co-hosts on the show are my mailman, my barber and my two buddies who have been fellow Red Sox season ticket holders with me for the last 20 years.

The studio is located in the Unified Arts building on the campus of Brookline High School, Dukakis' alma mater. This is to be Duke's ninth straight year on our hour-long show and he's always our favorite guest. Duke had never been on a show discussing sports before ours. This didn't stop me from inviting him or from him accepting.

Duke eats supper with his wife, Kitty, at their home and then walks to the show, traversing the same Brookline ground he's walked on for more than 80 years. One of my co-hosts, Joe McLaughlin, nicknamed Uncle Joe, whispers to me, "It's not like him to be late for anything." Joe knows Duke and Kitty well, as he has been their mailman for over two decades. Duke and Uncle Joe are from generations where "fashionably late" means being half an hour early. I'm concerned. It's the summer of 2021 and we're still knee deep in the pandemic. I hope that Duke or Kitty hasn't taken ill.

Dukakis is 88 years old. How rare is that? The current U.S. population consists of only .08 percent of males the age of 88. I try to call him, but I get a voice mail. I frantically email him, which, in the modern age of communication, is not where you head when frantic. The show's producer comes into the studio and says we have to start taping. The air is sucked out of the room, maybe because co-host Tim Hoey takes a big gasp of disappointment.

Hoey, who would give you the shirt off his back as well as take one off someone else if you needed it, is a maintenance supplies salesman. He comes from a huge blue-collar Irish family in the section of Boston called Jamaica Plain, or JP. I nicknamed him, *JP's First Son*. Everybody knows a Hoey. If you get jammed up in Boston, it's best to throw out the Hoey name as quickly as possible. For Tim to be hanging out with Dukakis is big in his circles. For that matter, it is for all of us.

Each year when I book the date of the show, I email the fellas using our nickname for Dukakis, *The Duke,* as the subject line. Every guy from Massachusetts has a nickname. It's a sign of endearment. Most of them have multiple nicknames. I think it's a state law. If you're an asshole, you only have that one nickname. I've had many nicknames in my life. Kermit, Kermy, Scooter. Scotty is used most often. So calling Michael Dukakis a nickname, whether it's the Governor or the Duke, is the ultimate sign of respect and certification that he's one of us.

We get through the show, minus Duke, as if it was a group counseling session for widowers, missing every aspect of Duke's appearance. We leave the studio, walk outside and are greeted by a loud voice from the darkness. "You guys locked out the Governor." Startled, I search through the darkness for the voice. "What?" I scream. A middle-aged guy comes out of the shadows. He's an MBTA employee who coordinates the public buses at the next-door T stop. "The Governor couldn't get into the building," he says. As I grow sicker by the milli-second, I ask again, "What?"

"Yeah, he came around six-thirty and couldn't get in. We talked for a while and then he started walking home." I look at the fellas in total disbelief at what had happened. "Was he mad?" I asked.

"No, he was fine and said to tell Scott to set up another time for him to be on the show." Stunned, I say, "Okay, thanks." We walk away and he screams through the darkness, "I wish he was still governor. Baker's a bum."

A few weeks later, I reschedule the Duke. I email him to ask if he wants Joe to pick him up.

Scott, I am still walking at least a mile a day so I will get there on my own. Just make sure the front door is unlocked. Mike.

We have multiple conversations with maintenance. Russ Stevens, another co-host, will be stationed out front to greet the Duke. Russ works for a think tank at MIT. He has two nicknames, *Professor* and *The Voice of Reason*. Russ' first job coming out of Dartmouth College was working on the Duke's presidential campaign. To be discussing politics with the Duke, as a peer, is clearly a special experience for him.

Joe and I get to the show early and the same MBTA employee is at the front of the building holding the door open. I immediately go into defense mode, as if I was in front of a police officer explaining my alibi. I tell the T worker everything is set and Russ will be waiting for him. He looks at Joe and me quite seriously and says, "I'm just going to stay here until the Governor comes like I promised him. Also, my wife was pissed I didn't get a selfie with him."

Dukakis made it into the studio and we had a great show. Every time he arrives, he always seems to appear out of nowhere, suddenly strolling in from behind the green screen curtain at the back of the studio and sporting the energy of a Dad entering a room with a lit birthday cake. Duke proceeds to tell us story after story about topics ranging from the Red Sox to his political service to the human condition. He exhibits a strong memory that spans all of his eight-plus decades.

For a show that normally has all of us talking over each other about Boston sports, we sit there silently and happily consume all of the Duke's words. I'm 55 years old and talking Red Sox is like breathing to me. But when Duke has the floor, I just sit back and listen. This man has been a role model for millions of people across the country.

Duke's appearances on the show are infamous for going well over the allotted hour. Each time, the director can be heard from the control room yelling for us to wrap it up. The show's producer comes into the studio and uses every hand-gesture known to man to direct us to shut it down. I'm pretty sure he flipped us more than two middle fingers. I ignore them all. We are honored to be sharing a table with such an extraordinary and accomplished man as he shares his great wealth of knowledge with a natural exuberance. I won't stop the Duke from talking. He will stop when he needs to go home to Kitty. No sooner.

After the show, Joe asked him if he needed a ride home. Duke said, "The T guy said he would be waiting outside to drive me home." Of course he did.

The Silent Generation Speaks

"Scott, I can't understand how anyone can be anything but honest. I was brought up to believe that honesty wasn't a choice, it was the way you lived your life. You tell the truth. That is non-negotiable. You do what's right. It's not that hard, I've never understood lying," Duke says with passion during the show.

Who talks like that anymore? Why doesn't anyone act like that anymore?

Dukakis has never had a book written about him. How's that possible for someone who has been such a key political figure in the last 50 years? Seemingly everyone who has had 15 minutes of political fame has a book. Former Vice-President Dan Quayle wrote his own autobiography called *Standing Firm*. Most of the book is probably misspelled.

I sent Duke an email explaining my thoughts about writing a book with him. "Governor, it's not going to be a biography," I wrote. There's 13 pages on Wikipedia where one can get their fix of Dukakis facts. He replied, "Scott, I am happy to help in any way I can, but I would feel a lot better if something like this involved more than just me." Humble as always.

How humble is the Duke? In 2014, Boston's South Station was renamed *The Governor Michael S. Dukakis Transportation Center at South Station*. I'm betting even the most diehard Dukakis groupies didn't know that. During the ceremony to unveil the new name, Dukakis surprisingly announced he "wasn't in favor of the move and doesn't think the name will catch on. This will be the first and last time my name is mentioned." Oh yeah, and thanks for the honor. I'll be here all week, have the veal.

"Scott, how many different names have we had for the Boston Garden?" Duke asked on *The Grandstanders*. "But it's still called the

Boston Garden. Don't get me wrong, I was grateful for the notice." Yeah, sure sounded like it. The people who attended the ceremony that day must have been really glad they missed lunch for that. Let's welcome to the stage our honored guest, Debbie Downer. I wasn't there, but I assume after Dukakis spoke, the skies opened up and drenched the lot of them. But he was right. Nobody has ever called it anything but South Station since. Shocker.

I was heading to Georgia on vacation with my wife, Adrienne, to stay at her best friend's beach house when I received a voice message from Dukakis' regarding the book. Once we arrived, I called him back to discuss it further. There was no answer, just a recorded request to leave a message on what was clearly an ancient answering machine. His outgoing message sounded like a tinny, boarding announcement from Grand Central station. *Hello, crackle, crack, not home, crack, crackle, message, crack. Beeeep.*

My phone rang a few hours later. "Hello, I received a call from this number and I could not make out any of the message," said the man on the other line with an answering machine that belonged in the Smithsonian. Hello, Governor, this is Scott. "Where are you?" he asked abruptly. I'm in Savannah, Georgia. "What are you doing there for?" he demanded in an upward pitch. By the time I got to the the word *vacation* in my explanation, I was already looking around trying to figure out what the hell I was doing there for. Wise older folks have the ability to make you question all your decisions. This was the New Englander coming out in him. New Englanders get personally offended if you leave the area unless someone dies and you're heading to a funeral. If you move out of the area, you might as well have died.

Dukakis went on to explain that he has a cousin "days younger" than him living in Savannah and that Kitty and he will be visiting in a few months. Of course he would. I guess it's alright for Kitty and him to go, but I head South, and it's the Spanish Inquisition. There might be six degrees of separation from Kevin Bacon, but it feels like it's no more than two degrees for the Duke. Makes sense. The man believed in personally canvassing each neighborhood of the area he would serve in a campaign. This might get you an ice cream cone at a smorgasbord in Methuen, but you'd need a whole lot of sneakers to cover the entire country.

Not only is Dukakis is a dying breed of politician, he's also a member of a dying generation. Dukakis was born in 1933, smack dab in the middle of a generation referred to as the Silent Generation, defined as those born between 1925-1945. These were the children of the Great Depression. That will keep you humble. Sadly, people born in the 1930s will all be gone soon except for those few centurions who will inevitably be told on their landmark birthday that they don't look anywhere near 100 years old. Hopefully, this keeps and we'll never get to that point in our civilization where someone who has survived a century of living will be trolled for looking their age. But I wouldn't bet on it.

All the knowledge and life experience, skill and contribution, work ethic and personal responsibility that the Silent Generation stalwartly infused into their communities is disappearing right along with them. When that old-time bakery that faithfully served Nona's secret family recipes for over 50 years finally closes, it'll probably be replaced by an eyebrow-threading salon. Sounds yummy.

When these family patriarchs and matriarchs disappear, their humanity and true empathy goes with them: The lending of an ear, the heartfelt thoughts and prayers, the not asking if there's anything they can do, but just doing it. There's a 100-year gap between that and today's phony-baloney words written in a tweet and punctuated and with an emoji.

You know your generation is humble when pretty much everyone thinks the generations go from The Greatest Generation directly to the Baby Boomers, skipping right over you. And you're still living! Now, that's keeping a low profile. Maybe they need a

Silent Generation t-shirt. A meme? Emoji? No member of the Silent Generation was president of the U.S. until Joe Biden, who was born in 1942. That was playing it a bit close to the wire. If Biden didn't win, an entire generation would never have had a representative as president, not that anyone would have noticed. I'm Generation X, so I'll mention it to them.

The Silents are noted for forming the leadership of the civil rights movement and creating the rock and roll music of the 1950s and 1960s. That's impressive stuff on a generational resume. Martin Luther King, Jr., all four Beatles, Elvis, Bill Russell, Hank Aaron, Mister Rogers, and Bruce Lee were Silents. Muhammad Ali, Shirley Temple, Bob Dylan, Johnny Cash, Aretha Franklin, Mickey Mantle, Mick Jagger, Jack Nicholson, and Evil Knievel were as well. Ironically enough, it seems like we've spent our whole lives watching and listening to the Silent Generation. And in a blink of an eye, they'll all be gone. What will we do after that?

We've decided I'm going to write a book where Duke and I sit at his kitchen table and talk, just like we do on my show. Let's see where it takes us. His words and mine. The End.

A few weeks later, I ring the doorbell to Duke's house and look over to a sign that reads, "Welcome to Mike and Kitty's house." The Duke answers and I happily walk into that old bakery.

Kerman family picture with Governor Dukakis
at ice cream smorgasbord fundraiser.

Duke and Kitty with The Grandstanders Live Show!

Duke and Scott at the television studio.

Duke and The Grandstanders.

Duke and Scott on stairs at Unified
Arts Building in Brookline, MA.

Duke with Scott on The Grandstanders.

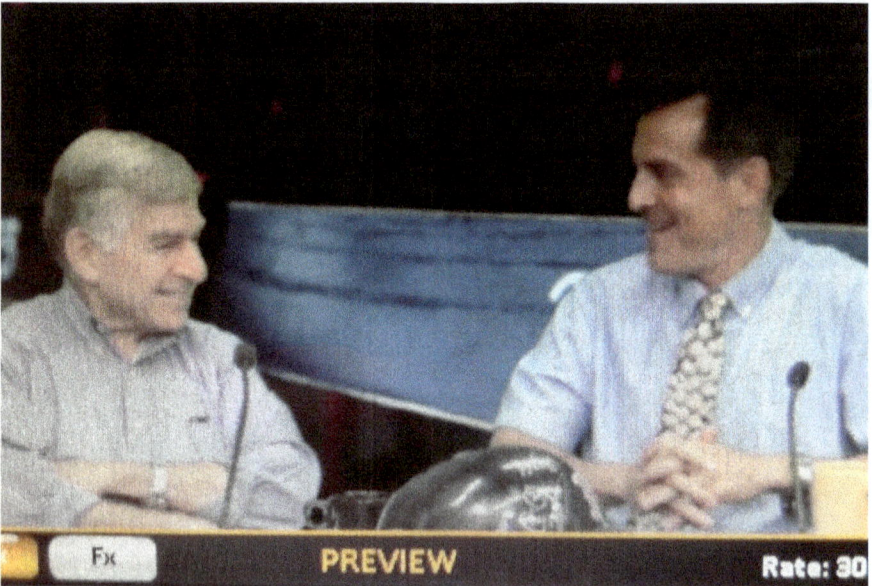

Duke with Scott on The Grandstanders.

Pull Up A Chair

The Dukakis' live in a large two-family Victorian home on a pleasant and quiet, tree-lined street in Brookline, a town in Massachusetts that sits right next door to Boston. The ancient wooden floorboards of Duke's front porch buckle as I walk up to the front door. Damn, someone's going to break their neck one of these days. I ring the doorbell and Duke answers with a big smile and warm greeting.

He leads me to the kitchen where we sit down. Duke has never forgotten my first name once in all these years. I don't take it for granted. I had an uncle who always called me Steve. No one ever bothered to correct him. I never mentioned it because I didn't want to embarrass him. To this day, I still turn around if someone screams out, "Hey Steve!"

The kitchen is quaint and has a simple table that sits near the window overlooking the back yard. A dog starts barking in the other room, a "cocker doodle" says the Duke. If the Duke doesn't like you, he never mentions you by name. He goes into the other room to quiet "that dog" down.

"Since I was nine years old and had a paper route, I've always had an interesting relationship with dogs," he says as he sits back down. He would like to send "that dog" to a shelter, but Kitty wants to keep it. The dog stays for now. Kitty is unable to attend to the dog as she's under the weather and is in bed upstairs.

"Scott, I'm not comfortable having a book solely about me. Can I just be part of it?" Duke repeats what he said to me on the phone, neither time with great conviction. It's like when someone is having a birthday party and they say 'no presents'. It sounds good, if that's what they want. Until you arrive.

Welcome, let me take your coat. Is there anything else I should take? Are you sure? We have a table over there if you have anything.

25

*Yes, the big one in the middle of the room with shiny lights and the **For Presents Only** sign.*

Duke will repeat the paper boy story again as the dog keeps barking. My father repeated stories many times in his later years and I enjoyed them as if I was hearing them for the first time. Duke repeating the story has the same effect. As a comedian most of my adult life, I've told some of the same bits thousands of times. Politicians have their canned speeches they make at every political event. The most successful comedians and politicians can do their *schtick* and make the audience feel like it's the first time every time.

Dukakis' last year as governor of Massachusetts was 1991. Like great athletes of the past, if you were around when they were at the top of their game, they're always a magical figure to you. If I say the name Dukakis to someone, there's no confusion as to whom I'm talking about.

If Duke had been an actor in an old television series, he would be busy appearing at Comic Con events and autograph shows across the country. Everyone in line to see him would be over 50 and armed with photos to sign of him sitting on a military tank wearing the infamous helmet. Customers would pay extra for him to inscribe: "Tanks for your support".

It has been said that you should never try to meet your heroes, lest they be found to have feet of clay. Despite Duke's age, if you were to see him on the street, you would know right away who it is. He still looks like Michael Dukakis. Duke is the most approachable famous person I've ever met, if he hasn't approached you first. When speaking to the Duke, he looks you directly in the eyes and listens. He asks follow-up questions and engages in conversation. He makes you feel special. How many people in your life can you say that about?

Where are you from? Where did you go to school? What do you do for a living? Asking these questions to a complete stranger may sound quite normal, but it's Governor Michael Dukakis asking them, making life memories for someone on the corner of Beacon Street and Harvard Street.

Even if you didn't know who he was, he looks like a man who was 'somebody' back in the day. Maybe he was a doctor, or managed your parent's portfolio, or was almost President of the United States. Something.

"My dear mother was an unusual woman who came to this country from Greece when she was nine years old. She was the first Greek girl to ever go unescorted to college in the United States."

I nod. Clearly, my face isn't reacting appropriately to this extraordinary achievement. I'm thinking, did every Greek girl check in daily with Greek headquarters to update them on her firsts? Was there a first lady of Greek immigrants to sign an apartment lease? "Scott, going unescorted was a big thing back in the day," Duke says in an older person "aren't you cute as a button" way. "That was a startling sight in those prim days," he states. Sounds good. He convinced me. It's not verifiable then or now, but why not? Is there any other Greek son of immigrants claiming this title for his mom right now? If she was an insurance agent, she would surely have this plaque on an office wall supporting the narrative.

My father and my uncle Irving used to say they played semi-pro baseball. I thought that was very cool growing up and used to brag to my friends. Later, I realized it was probably what we now call Little League. Didn't matter. Did your father play semi-pro? I don't think so.

Duke is a small man in height and weight. No more than five-foot, seven-inches tall. He didn't come from great wealth or political power, unlike his presidential opponent George H.W. Bush. He had to build up everything about himself—his family, his friends, their achievements, and his own. If you compared his rise to prominence to making a cake, Dukakis would have started with a couple spoons of sugar, where H.W. Bush just needed to find a knife to cut it.

Duke had to create a life narrative so big that he could stand tall in any room, convincing everyone that there were a lot of "firsts" in his camp. Before Google and the word "vetting," you could say a lot to people and they would buy it. Just have a neat appearance and don't have too much alcohol on your breath and you're hired. We live in a country where everyone pumps their tires. People on Facebook portray perfect families and lives. A former neighbor of mine posted pictures ad nauseam with her and her husband acting all lovey-dovey. *Cupid's Couple* she coined themselves. One problem, she was screwing the high school football coach *and* baseball coach, depending on what sport her kid was playing at the time. I was kind of hoping the husband was hanging out with the Home Economics teacher during the holidays.

Duke's reading *The Boston Globe*. "Why has that guy refused to concede the election? He's nuts, to be perfectly frank," Duke says in an exasperated tone. I'm not sure of much in life, but I'm pretty positive "that guy" is Donald Trump.

"Scott, isn't that part of the political process? You don't want to do it. You don't want to concede that you lost. It's not pleasant. I wasn't under any illusions I was going to win that thing on election day. All of the polls on the week before election day seemed to indicate that Bush was going to beat me. Once they count the votes and, if you've lost, you gotta stand up, concede the election, and publicly accept what happened," Duke says in a strong tone.

I'm thinking, maybe you accept publicly losing a two-man race to become the most important and powerful person in the world on that one night. But how do you privately come to grips with that defeat for the rest of of your life?

Since the death of Republican Bob Dole in 2021, Duke is the oldest living major party presidential nominee candidate who has lost that election. Al Gore, John Kerry, Mitt Romney, Hillary Clinton and the Duke are the only living presidential nominees of their party who were never president. Only this small group is left to share that experience. These are huge names in the last 50 years of U.S. politics. You all want to go out to breakfast? Let's meet at Zaftig's in Brookline. I'm paying.

Even if you put the defeat in some corner of your emotional library, it still remains a lifetime cloud hanging over your head. Each day is another chance to be reminded of the loss, by pretty much everyone you come into contact with.

"I'll have a cruller and a coffee." "That will be $4.75. Hey, I know you, didn't you lose the presidency?"

We know it's never one person who loses the race by themselves. Just ask Red Sox First Baseman, Bill Buckner. During game six of the 1986 World Series, the ball passed between his legs allowing the winning run by the New York Mets. Most people think that Bill Buckner lost the Red Sox the World Series on that play. Nope. There was a deciding Game Seven, a game where the Red Sox were leading 3-0 in the bottom of the sixth inning and blew the lead to lose to the Mets 8-5 and the Series. Buckner didn't lose anything for the Red Sox. Had he fielded the grounder properly, Game 6 would have gone to extra innings.

The details of the World Series didn't matter for Buckner. He was trolled unmercifully like no one has ever seen to this day. That was before the Internet! The first line of his obituary was written as soon as the ball had passed his legs.

From <u>ESPN.Com</u>: *Bill Buckner, the longtime major leaguer whose error in the 1986 World Series for years lived in Red Sox infamy, died Monday. He was 69.*

Buckner had 2,715 hits over a 22 season career and a lifetime batting average of .289—borderline Hall of Fame numbers. You have to be a baseball junkie to look past that one moment of Buckner's career to appreciate the outstanding body of work. Nobody has done that.

Dukakis served as governor of Massachusetts for three terms and is the longest serving governor in Massachusetts' history. He was nominated by the Democratic Party for president in 1988. That's quite a body of work. You don't have to be a political junkie to look past his presidential defeat to appreciate his exceptional success in public service. Will you? But more importantly, will Dukakis?

Imaginable Losses

The Duke had become familiar with great loss far before that first Tuesday in November 1988. His older brother and lone sibling, Stelian Dukakis, was riding a bicycle in Brookline in 1973 when he was struck by a vehicle in a hit and run. He was 42.

Boston Globe *obituary, July 30, 1973: Stelian P. Dukakis, 42, of 198 St. Paul Street, Brookline, the brother of former state Rep. Michael Dukakis, died yesterday at Beth Israel Hospital. Mr. Dukakis, a government professor at Boston State College, had been in critical condition at the hospital since March 17, when he was injured by a hit and run automobile near his home. He was a former schoolteacher in the North Attleboro school system. Mr. Dukakis was twice defeated in the past two years during* elections *for Brookline's Board of Selectmen. He was a former assistant city manager in Waltham and Malden. In addition to his brother, Mr. Dukakis leaves his parents, Dr. Panos and Euterpe Dukakis of 454 Huntington Ave, Boston.*

In all the times I've spoken to Duke over the years, he's only mentioned his brother's accident once in passing. Duke was finishing up lunch when I arrived on this day. He asked me if I wanted a Greek pastry, and I never say "no" to a dessert. He began fiddling in the kitchen to get the dessert on the plate. It felt like a good time to mention it.

You only touched briefly about your brother? "My brother, it's a sad story," Duke said in a barely audible tone." Stelian died in 1973 while riding a bicycle, right? I asked. "He was on Winchester Street and some guy came along and hit him. In those days, we didn't know a lot about mental health," he said.

As he placed the Greek pastry in front of me, I'm thinking, I didn't mention anything about mental health. I'll focus on dessert in a bit.

"In fact, when Kitty started having these recurring depressions out of the clear blue sky... Kitty. Depression. Whatever. She was in her early forties. It was frustrating as hell. It was rough. She went to a psychiatrist. It never made a difference. I was at the end of my rope. Then one last try. Go see Charlie Welch, Mass General. Electro Compulsive Therapy. ECT. It was a miracle."

The next question flew out of my mouth. Did your brother have mental illness? "Yes, he had a nervous breakdown and was institutionalized. He went to a place in the North Shore. I was in high school at the time. Stelian was in college. He recovered, but he was never the same," Duke said.

Duke looks down at the floor and rubs his hands like he was washing them for a minute's time. "Stelian goes back to Bates and was interested in public service. He gets hit by a car. People heard the impact and see a guy on a bike lying in the gutter on Winchester Street," a frustrated Duke says.

Do you remember going to the hospital? "Yes. I can't tell you what injuries he had. He's the reason I went to Swarthmore. Stelian had said, would you like to go to Swarthmore? But I thought it was a girls' school. Next thing I know, I'm in Pennsylvania with the cows at Swarthmore."

How did the loss of your brother affect you? "You have to keep living your life, but I lost my brother whom I loved dearly," He tears up. "It was very, very tough. We were very close. I really loved him. Three years older. He was my big brother, and I kind of followed him around," he looks down at the floor again and rubs his fingers.

I didn't mean to make the Duke cry. It's the last thing I wanted to do. I put my hand on his shoulder. It doesn't matter if you lost a loved one fifty minutes ago or fifty years ago. The pain sits on the surface of your emotions ready to rear itself up at any moment.

Governor, from all accounts I have read, the hit and run driver was never identified. Did you ever find out who hit your brother? "Yes, a year later." Is that right? I look around the room for a moment. I wasn't ready for that answer.

Was it a male or female? "Male." Did you know him, or had you ever heard of him? "No." Why didn't you have him prosecuted? "I discussed it with some people and we decided to let it go," he said as his voice trailed off.

I was going to ask further questions about his brother's situation when the phone rings. I'll have to revisit that topic at a later time. I'm immediately brought back to the 1980s as he picks up his portable landline phone. It's probably left over from a *Dukakis for President* phone bank.

Duke intently tries to answer it and he ends up answering and hanging up on his daughter simultaneously. The answering machine on the phone decides to get involved. It makes that harsh, beeping noise I hadn't heard in at least twenty years. I think it might detonate.

Duke excuses himself as he goes to the other room to look for his daughter's number, probably on an index card somewhere.

He comes back into the kitchen and calls her back. He waits awhile and leaves a message, or did he miss hearing the beep? "Those damn answering machines," he said. I'm sure she'll call back, I said. He gives me a big smile. Duke doesn't sweat the small stuff at all.

Kitty walks into the the kitchen and stands at the doorway. "Michael, where's mother and father?" she says as her voice cracks. "They're gone Kitty, we're a mother and father," Duke says. Looking perplexed, Kitty says "OK" and heads back upstairs to bed. We just look at each other for a moment.

I was brought up in family of eight with lots of aunts, uncles, cousins, etc., around the house. I'm used to relatives walking into rooms and talking like it was a sitcom before making an exit. I'm always just waiting for the neighbor to pop his head out the window and begin singing show tunes.

How did you balance being a Governor with your family life? "Making sure I devoted good time to my family, no politics on Sunday. My standard rule. Home for dinner every night, almost without exception. It was very important. Did I go out at night after supper at times, yeah. But I wanted to be home with Kitty and the kids for supper."

How about when you ran for President? "Except for the Presidential campaign, and then Friday was my day off. Every Friday. It was non-negotiable. Very important to me." Duke said. "No phones. I would not have changed it for the world. No exceptions," Duke said. He lightly bangs the table. "Dinner at six o'clock every night."

Growing up in the 1970s and '80s, pretty much everyone in my neighborhood had a home-cooked dinner as a family at around six o'clock. It really was a sacred time of the day. I can't remember ever fighting with my five siblings at the dinner table. We saved that for the other twenty-three hours.

"We will be married sixty years this June," he says proudly. They met for the first time while Duke was running the Boston Marathon in 1951 as a senior at Brookline High School. Kitty, who was a freshman at Brookline High, offered him water as he ran on Beacon Street.

"Kitty was already married once before, I caught her on the rebound," Duke laughs. Kitty married businessperson John Chaffetz in 1957. Kitty and Chaffetz had one son, John, who was later adopted by Dukakis. After four years, Kitty's marriage ended in divorce. Kitty's former husband later remarried and had a son, Jason Chaffetz, who became a Republican Congressman from Utah.

"I still don't understand why it was John Chaffetz. I don't know why she was attracted to the guy," Duke says, as he looks at me like he needs some buddy affirmation. I blurt out, "Me neither, who knows?" Duke nods his approval.

"It wasn't a successful marriage, fortunately for me. Scott, what did she see in him?" Ahh... I had not heard of John Chaffetz until thirty seconds ago, so I do a big shoulder shrug. Duke shakes his head in disgust. Another emotion, like loss of a loved one, that has no expiration date: Jealousy.

It's been over sixty years and Duke can't understand why his wife Kitty would have ever had a relationship with another man before they started dating. If Duke still has these unanswered questions, then delving into a defeat to be President of the United States is going to be quite interesting.

My Fellow Americans

"What are the things that you can't see that are important? I would say justice, truth, humility, service, compassion, love. You can't see any of those, but they're guiding lights of a life." (President Jimmy Carter)

My buddy Pete MacGillivray's mom died. She was a classmate of Duke and the same age as him. Pete is part of *The Grandstanders*. He's a barber and he owns *Mac's* barber shop in Brookline. He succeeds his father and grandfather at the barber shop. Three generations of 'Mac's' cutting men's hair in Brookline. That's a lot of DNA on the floor over the last ninety plus years. Pete will cut your hair and help you work out any life issues you have in fifteen minutes time. Then you're out the door to figure out the rest of your life on your own.

Pete's a tall, handsome, giant of a man. A James Garner type. Pete either likes you or he doesn't. No middle ground. I went to his barber shop to pay my condolences. I walked in and gave him a big hug. He's sixty-five years old and he'll be asked at this point to live the rest of his life without his mother. When you get older, you're set in your ways. He's lived a long time to have to adjust now to not having his mom in his life.

"Scott, one of the things I'll miss most about my mom was that she laughed at all my jokes, some of which really weren't very funny," Pete said with a tear in one eye and a glint of humor in the other. "I'll miss hearing her voice. It took me five years to get over my father's death. I don't think I'll live long enough to get over this," said Pete.

Men of a certain age like Pete were taught from a young age to never cry and to keep their emotions to themselves. Show signs of any feelings and emotions and you were considered worthless and weak. Is that moisture coming from your eyes? No one cares if you were cutting onions. Down the Willie Wonka garbage chute for you!

1972 Democratic presidential candidate, Maine Senator Edward Muskie, allegedly shed tears in remarks outside the Manchester Union-Leader newspaper in response to criticism of his wife, an incident which forced Muskie to later withdraw from the race. Muskie denied that he cried and said reporters mistook melting snow on his cheeks for tears. It didn't matter. Senator Muskie, you've been eliminated from consideration. Brace for impact. Bye, bye. Presidents don't cry.

I recall seeing a *Politico* interview with the late Vice-President Walter Mondale, who won the Democratic nomination for President in 1984. Mondale was soundly defeated by incumbent President Ronald Reagan. Mondale paid a visit to Senator George McGovern, who more than 12 years earlier in 1972, had won the Democratic nomination. McGovern was trounced in the general election by the incumbent President Richard Nixon. This was the second biggest landslide in American history with an Electoral College total of 520 to 17.

McGovern won Massachusetts and the District of Columbia and that was it. He even lost his home state of South Dakota, which is hard to do seeing as he probably knew everyone who voted in the state personally. During the interview, Mondale said "I remember when, after I lost my race for President, I went to see George. Tell me how long it takes to get over a defeat of this kind?" Mondale asked. McGovern replied, "I'll call you when it happens."

I went over to Duke's house on a bitterly cold early February day. I walk to his home from my house, which takes about 20 minutes. February weather in Massachusetts comes under the heading of three categories: Really Shitty, Shitty, and Kinda Shitty. Today was the latter.

I stumble into the house away from the elements. As always, a big smile from Duke greets me as he takes the two jackets I'm wearing. Each time I come over, it feels like Duke is happier to see me. I say hello to Kitty as she heads up the stairs and we sit down at the kitchen table.

I no longer feel the Uncle Duke vibe. Now it's more a Grandpa Duke vibe. Both of my grandfathers had passed away before I was born. I'm more than happy to be grandparent-adopted. My goal this day is to watch Dukakis' 1988 Democratic National Convention acceptance speech with Duke. I'm hoping he will be receptive to watching it.

That night in '88, I was going to jump on a couple of open-mike, comedy nights to work out some new jokes, but instead stayed home to watch the Convention. My guy Michael Dukakis was to be nominated to be the Democratic candidate for the President of the United States. Bigger than Big! Do you personally know the current nominee for President? I don't think so.

Governor, I would like us to watch your DNC speech together, is that okay? "Sure, why not," Duke says. I brought my laptop and attempted to get WIFI. Yes, his WIFI username was Duke 5g. Knowing the answer, yet still asking the question: "Governor, any chance you remember your WIFI password?" Duke gives me the squint and head-to-the-side look. OK, we will watch it on my phone. I leaned the phone against the Lazy Susan on the kitchen table. Can you see alright? He nods and I press play. The video is a little grainy, but so are we.

It begins with Duke's cousin and Academy Award winning actress Olympia Dukakis introducing him. Olympia won the Academy Award for Best Supporting Actress the year prior in 1987 for the movie Moonstruck.

It was looking like it would be one hell of a couple of years for the Dukakis family from Greece. An Academy Award winner and a president of the United States. Most families are happy if they bought a new lawn mower in the last year.

I'm betting if you asked a thousand people if they would rather be president or win an Academy Award, the majority would pick winning the Oscar. Olympia passed away in 2021 at the age of eighty-nine years old. Duke adores his cousin Olympia.

Uncle Joe and I drove Duke home one night from a show and he spent the whole ride going on and on about Olympia. Usually when we've dropped him off at home, we stop the car, he says goodbye and hits the pavement at the same time. On this particular night, he spent thirty minutes more in the car waxing poetic about his *older* cousin.

I just noticed Duke never wears glasses. Not even to read. How many people don't wear reading glasses by the age of fifty? That's another trait that disappears with Duke's generation. Duke spent the first fifty plus years not staring at a computer every day, doing a hatchet job on his eyesight. Future generations will be wearing eyeglasses in the womb.

You don't wear glasses? "No, I don't need them for reading." How's that possible? "I just need them for distance sometimes. My mother who lived to ninety nine years old, only wore glasses at the very end." Governor, you have a hell of gene pool going.

His memory isn't as strong as his eyesight. Duke quickly asks me to stop the video. "Scott, I'm starting to forget things. My memory isn't what it used to be. Small things here and there." Trying to make him feel better I joke: So am I. I guess we're getting old.

It feels like he thought about it and decided to tell me this. Duke is very careful about what comes out of his mouth. He understands the power of words. I'm honored to be a person he's comfortable with enough to share such personal information. I don't take the responsibility lightly.

Thankfully, for the sake of the book and posterity purposes, I have many hours of video from our show together to turn to if needed.

If you're in your late eighties and have your wits about you, then you pretty much self diagnose. Yes, it's very likely that Duke is going down some kind of dementia road. But he looks in good shape and sounds great. His hairline is that of a ten year old. He's wearing a warm sweater with comfortable khaki pants and his legs are folded. How are *you* doing?

Is he going to expend a second getting poked and prodded by doctors to tell him something he can figure out at the kitchen table? Duke understands he's grown old as he's been present every second of the way. What was the other choice? As he says often, "So here we are."

Should I turn the video back on? Duke's staring at the still picture of Olympia on the video. I feel like he's transported himself back in time. I can't imagine what's going through his mind. When's the last time you watched it? "A while ago," he whispers.

I'm betting he probably watched it the next day after the speech and that's the last time. If you're of a certain age, thirty five years ago can still fall under the heading of "a while ago." Are you ready? He nods. Let's do this! I press play.

Pretty Good Speech

I watched the DNC speech twice in preparation for my visit. There are moments in your life where you realize that you may be the only person on the planet that's doing a particular act. Watching Dukakis' 1988 presidential acceptance speech feels like such a moment.

And we're going to win this race. We're going to win because we are the party that believes in the American dream. A dream so powerful that no distance of ground, no expanse of ocean, no barrier of language, no distinction of race or creed or color can weaken its hold on the human heart.

After we watched the speech for a few minutes, I asked him what he was feeling right now? "I'm just watching," he says. You could see Duke go into a trance, seemingly not blinking to take in every millisecond. He was staying focused and getting lost back in the moment.

July 21, 1988 was the pinnacle of Duke's professional and public life. He had just been nominated by the Democratic Party to be the candidate for president of the United States. He was speaking in front of an enthusiastic crowd and addressing the world on that Thursday night as a person who quite possibly, in a few months' time, could be elected to be the most powerful person in the world. Mind boggling to say the least.

Early in his speech, Dukakis mentions Henry Cisneros of Texas, Bob Matsui of California, Barbara Mikulski of Maryland, Mario Cuomo of New York, and Claude Pepper of Florida. Duke said he didn't remember who Claude Pepper was and he asked if I did? No. It's a cool name, though, if I ever need an alias. Duke laughs.

Pepper was a long-time Congressman from Florida who died six months after the Duke's speech at the age of 88, while still in office. Will we all be forgotten 30 years after our deaths? Will anyone remember Duke in 2055?

I would imagine our collective memories will continue to be shorter since people have stopped putting pictures in frames and hanging them up. Will people only remember loved ones when they receive a Facebook reminder from the past? What happens when FB goes kaput? Where will we go for memories and misinformation?

I can't guess how many politicians Duke has had conversations with over his political career, one that began 60 years ago after his election to the Massachusetts House of Representatives in 1963. Thousands for sure. How many people has he met and hands has he shaken? Over a million? Not out of the question. Safe bet no politician will ever have that on their life's resume again.

A handshake is a brief greeting or parting tradition in which two people grasp each other's like hand. During the pandemic, we were told that if you shook someone's hand it could be fatal, and the handshake was replaced by a fist bump. Can you imagine how many times Duke would have cracked his knuckles? *I'm voting for the pleasant guy with the Boston accent who's got a cast on both hands.*

Back to the speech, as the Duke lays it on thick to recognize Jesse Louis Jackson.

"A man who has lifted so many hearts with the dignity and the hope of his message throughout this campaign; a man whose very candidacy has said to every child, aim high; to every citizen, you count; to every voter, you can make a difference; to every American, you are a full shareholder in our dream.

What did you think of Jesse Jackson? Duke instantly blurted out "pain in the ass." Did you have to cut any deals with Jackson for his support? "No, but he always wanted the campaign to fly him in a private jet." Duke shakes his head in disgust.

For a man who rode the subway to work as governor, this was blasphemy. Duke would crawl on his hands and knees with *The Rock* on his back to his destination before paying for a private jet for himself, much less for someone else. "Jackson was always quite a difficult guy." Gloves are off. Here we go.

As we continue to watch, he speaks in a low tone, not to interrupt hearing himself speak. "Pretty good speech," he says. His face is almost touching the phone now, most likely so he can see it better, but it's as if he wants to jump into the phone and travel back in time. President Reagan is mentioned during the speech.

The American dream belongs to the privileged few and not to all of us. You tell them that the Reagan era is over and that a new era is about to begin.

Did you have a sense that Reagan had some form of dementia during the course of your campaign? "Reagan was a little dizzy in general," said the Duke. I laugh. Were you running against Reagan or Bush in 88? "Reagan."

Duke has been described his whole political life as closely guarded in his behavior and words. To some level, this is the person I've been speaking to regularly for fifteen years. Not anymore.

It's clear to me that Duke understands the time to articulate his thoughts is a running clock in the final quarter with no time outs. It seems like he doesn't have two shits to give anymore. As far as taking the high ground.

It's time to rekindle the American spirit of invention and of daring, to exchange voodoo economics for can-do economics, to build the best America by bringing out the best in every American.

"That was a really good line," says the Duke. I nod and we both smile.

And we're going make teaching a valued and honored profession again.

"Making teaching a valued profession again. Was there something going on at the time?" asks the Duke. Having been out of college for a year at the time of the speech, I had no idea. My family and I have always held teachers in a high regard. Growing up, if you saw a funeral with a long line down the street, chances are it was for a teacher.

"Why don't you look it up?" Duke says. OK. Feeling as if my grandfather just gave me a task, I search around the Internet for a mere ten seconds. "OK, what did you come up with?" Governor, that's all the time I get?

When Dukakis was born in 1933, radio, newspapers, telephone, and mail were the primary forms of communication used. Only forty percent of households owned a radio or telephone. Public libraries were serving seventy percent of the U.S population.

In 1933, if you were trying to find answers about a political hot topic '35 years ago', you would have been looking at the year 1898! It might have taken you ten years to discover the information. I couldn't figure out what teacher issue he was referring to in 1988 with my limited time window and all, but it sure hasn't gone well since. I read to Duke what I found:

'In a recent Merrimack College Teacher's Job Satisfaction Survey, a little more than half of teachers are satisfied with their jobs, and only twelve percent say they're "very satisfied" with their jobs, down from thirty-nine percent in 2012.'

Governor, all the teachers in the country should've voted for you."That's for sure," he says while nodding. "Everyone should have." We both nod.

Duke is like an old furnace. It takes time for him to heat up but once he gets going, it's a warm and comfortable place to be. Kitty walks into the kitchen in her bathrobe and sits at the table. I pause the speech.

I enjoy the three of us sitting at the kitchen table together. The former first lady of Massachusetts feels comfortable enough around me to hang out in her pajamas. I think this should be the new definition of being *in one's political circle.*

"Kitty had ECT yesterday," Duke says almost like a proud father. "She has them once every three months. She's doing pretty good for 87." He looks at her lovingly. I didn't know what to say. Awesome, Kitty, keep up the great work at psychotherapy. I chose to smile instead.

Electroconvulsive therapy (ECT) is a procedure done under general anesthesia in which small electric currents are passed through the brain, intentionally triggering a brief seizure. ECT seems to cause changes in brain chemistry that can quickly reverse symptoms of certain mental health conditions. (Mayo Clinic)

Kitty sits at the table and stares out the window. "It looks horrible out there," she says. "I'm going to go back upstairs." "OK, sweetie pie," says Duke. "Let's see if we can walk around three, promise?" Kitty makes an inaudible sound; gives Duke a look which screams, *that's not happening;* and gets up from the chair and leaves the kitchen. OK, back to watching the speech.

It's time to ask why it is that we have run up more debt in this country in the last eight years than we did in the previous 200; and to make sure it never happens again.

"What's the national debt currently?" he asks. Finally, a question I could check within the ten-second time limit. Over 31 trillion. "That's sounds like a lot of money," he jokes. The national debt when Duke was born was twenty-two billion. Not exactly chump change either for the time.

The greatest threat to our national security in this hemisphere is not the Sandinistas — it's the avalanche of drugs that is pouring into this country and poisoning our kids. It's not about overthrowing governments in Central America but creating jobs in Middle America. It's not about insider trading on Wall Street; it's about creating opportunity on Main Street.

"You don't hear much from the DEA these days," Duke says. Right, the guys who were always standing next to a table full of drugs, cash, and guns like it would soon be theirs. All the while wearing bad windbreakers, I said. Duke laughed.

It's about American values. Old-fashioned values like accountability and responsibility and respect for the truth.The kind of America that provides American workers and their families with at least 60 days' notice when a factory or plant shuts down.

"What were they doing, tossing them out?" Duke asked. I can't help but chuckle. I guess so, I said. Governor, you don't hear too much anymore about U.S. factories shutting down because lots of goods are made oversees now. "I would have kept a lot of those jobs here," Duke says with a clenched fist.

Time to see that young families in this country are never again forced to choose between the jobs they need and children they love.

"What's that in reference to?" asked Duke. I answer, childcare. It's clear by his body language that he's not interested in discussing childcare any further. That's a young person's game.

One of my college buddies had to take a second mortgage out on his condo in New York City to afford childcare. Rich folks' answer to childcare is called a live-in nanny as the child transitions into boarding school.

This fall we're going to be hearing a lot of Republican talk about how well some neighborhoods and some regions of this country are doing; about how easy it is for some families to buy a home or to find childcare or to pay their doctor bills or to send their children to college.

Governor, I don't think most current working-class families think it's easy to do any of these things. "The Republicans have always been out of touch," says Duke.

It is the idea of community. The kind of community that binds us here tonight. It is the idea that we are in this together; that regardless of who we are or where we come from or how much money we have — each of us counts. And that by working together to create opportunity and a good life for all — all of us are enriched — not just in economic terms, but as citizens and as human beings.

"Not a bad speech. Not a bad speech at all. With one mistake." So, what's missing? "We didn't anticipate. We should have been ready with that crime stuff. There was the death penalty and all of that." I stop the video as I can see he's on a roll.

"Look Scott, the homicide rate in Greater Houston was six times the homicide rate of Massachusetts. Bush was from Houston, and I was from Boston. They have the death penalty in Texas; Massachusetts does not. And I never said that. Don't ask me why. For the life of me I don't understand it. What was I thinking? What was I thinking!" Duke yelled.

Governor, to this day, do you think that changes things? That if you had relayed that particular message to the American public, it would it have swayed the election? "Yes, most definitely. I would have won."

You wish that you had included that in this speech? "Yeah," says the Duke. He's now fired up and percolating. So, you think about it still? Duke's voices it strongly: "Yes. Six times the homicide rate. Six times!" As he shakes his head.

It's clear to me that for 36 years and counting, Duke has been second-guessing his actions that might have contributed to his loss for the presidency. And I thought Vitamin C pills were tough to swallow.

Governor, how does the loss of the presidential election compare to the loss of a loved one? Taking into account that you would not have played a role in a loved one's death; it's just part of life. Not in your control.

Duke looks down to the floor and takes quite a long moment to respond to the question. He speaks with his chin leaning on his chest. "It's painful. Yeah. Are you disappointed in yourself? Yeah. But no, it doesn't compare to losing someone you love. It's different. But six times!"

Does Anyone Like Mitt Romney?

S*cott, Unfortunately, Kitty is not doing well. I'll keep you posted over the next few days. Mike*

Two days later: *Kitty is feeling better. How about the start of next week? Mike*

My wife and I have owned a beach cottage in Maine for 20 years. On the street we walk heading to the beach is another cottage owned by an older gentleman named Frank who is in his eighties.

Every day for over 20 years, Frank has sat on his front porch on an old wooden rocking chair. We always make sure to wave to Frank on our way back and forth. Every once in awhile, Frank asks me to bring his barrels in from the street and I'm happy to do it. "Thanks, kid," he says. Who in their mid-fifties doesn't like to be called "kid"?

Throughout the many summers, we would notice more and more people, locals to tourists alike, visiting with Frank on his porch. They would sit next to him or gather on the stairs and share their life stories and problems.

Frank's a soft-spoken man with a very reserved Maine personality. He listens and offers some words of encouragement to his visitors. But he mostly listens as he looks toward the beach and rocks his chair. It's like *Field of Dreams*. If you build a cottage near the beach and you sit an old man down on a rocking chair, they will come. They will come on the porch for reasons they can't even fathom, not knowing for sure why they're doing it. They'll arrive at Frank's porch as innocent as children, longing for loved ones who have passed on, who offered a comforting ear and voice. Duke is my Frank.

I never ring the Duke's doorbell even one minute early. I'm exactly on time for each visit, which is two o'clock on the button on this day. I walk around his neighborhood like a stalker waiting to ring the bell. I came a few minutes early once and he pronounced, "You're early," in a tone someone would typically use to admonish you if you're late. I'm not doing that again!

Duke greets me at the door with his welcoming smile and we head to the kitchen. Wearing his attire of button-down shirt, khaki pants, and sneakers. Duke will wear the occasional sweater on top of his dress shirt. He was known for wearing sweaters during his daily televised updates during the infamous Blizzard of 1978 as Governor.

New Englanders over 50 years old who experienced that once-in-a-lifetime snowstorm, never miss the opportunity to bring it up. You could be asking someone to "pass the salt" and they will say how it reminds them of how much salt they had to lay down to get through the Blizzard of 78.

Looking as comfortable and content as an older man can possibly be, we get settled at the kitchen table. Lots of research backs up the belief that people are happier as they age into their later years. Duke builds on the theory. On this day, I hope to get his thoughts on some famous modern-day political figures.

He's anxious to get started, as if it we were on a game show. The joyful atmosphere that engulfs the kitchen is palpable. It has a feeling that after we're done for the day, we should fire up the barbecue, crack open some beers, and start playing cards.

In my experience, there is an innocence that comes with people in their eighties and nineties. It's as if they've reverted to childhood with their excitement and enthusiasm of all things new and old.

I start with former President Bill Clinton. Clinton was the governor of Arkansas, and the the keynote speaker at the 1988 convention. You could say that the Duke gave Clinton his jump-start on a national stage.

Clinton's speech was long and boring. The convention producers were waving their arms and flashing a red light for Clinton to end the speech, but he ignored them and went on and on. The DNC crowd gave a mock cheer when Clinton said, "In conclusion."

"I liked Bill a lot. Worked together as governors. Smart guy politically and intellectually. He was quite impressive the way he worked with people. He had great skills. He was a remarkable guy in so many ways, coming out of rural Arkansas. He was very bright, and I thought he was a good president under interesting circumstances," Duke said.

Did you consider Clinton to be your running mate as opposed to Senator Lloyd Bentsen (TX)? "I don't think so," Were there any conversations with Clinton? "Not that I recall. It's not that we didn't know each other and like each other. It was a good, close friendship, and I liked him a lot. A talented guy. We shared a common approach."

Governor, he seemed to fit the suit. He was a southern politician. Up and coming. I'm just surprised he wasn't worthy of a meeting. "I never considered it."

It's crazy to think that Clinton would be president four years later and Dukakis never gave a thought to even having a discussion with him about the VP possibilities. Maybe Clinton wasn't considered because Bentsen balanced the ticket as a Washington insider, strange as that is to say in today's political environment. Who knows.

Let's go to Hillary Clinton. "I like her. Very bright. I admire her very much and she's very able and cares very deeply about the country. I can't say I've had many opportunities to speak with her."

Did she reach out to you before either of her runs for president? Duke shakes his head. Did that bother you? It's not like it's a long list of people who are living who have been the Democratic nominee for president. "It would have been nice to speak to her," he says as he kicks into politician mode for a moment. Somewhere, Hillary just felt a stitch in her side.

How does Hillary not do that? One phone call to show respect for the Duke, the Democratic Party, and the nominees before her. I believe Duke in his prime would have beaten Hillary for the Democratic nomination and trounced Trump in 2016. Duke has plenty to offer as far as advice. I don't know why she couldn't have spared five minutes. She could have done it from the bathroom for God's sake.

How about John Kerry? He was your lieutenant governor from 1982-1984. Kerry was the senator from Massachusetts. He won the Democratic nomination for president in 2004 and lost to George W. Bush. What went wrong for Kerry in the presidential election? "Another tough one to figure out why he lost."

Were you surprised that he lost to George W.? "Yes. He should have beat him. I feel that giving him specific responsibility as Lieutenant Governor helped him. He's done important stuff in his career."

Pardon me if I use a cuss word in the house but let me bring up a Republican. Duke laughs. For my whole childhood, as the fourth of sixth children, (middle child alert), my contribution to the house was humor. Duke has become a receptive audience, like being with my father back in the day. I never miss an opportunity to make him smile.

What do you think of Mitt Romney? You have similar backgrounds. You were both governors of Massachusetts, (Romney from 2003-2007) and you both were nominees of your party for president and lost. What was your relationship with Romney?

"Not much of one. He was a different Republican from many Republicans of today. He's a liberal Republican and continues to stand out in that way and for that, I have lots of respect for him."

This is how a good, decent person acts, and answers a question. Romney could take notice.

In the documentary called *Mitt,* Romney is shown making a speech in 2002 in Los Angeles ripping into Dukakis. Not for any reason I can figure, but just because Romney's an asshole.

Romney: *You know I get beaten up, that goes with the territory, and I have looked, by the way, at what happened to anybody in this country who loses as the nominee of their party. Who loses the general election they become a loser for life.* **Romney makes the L sign**. *That's it. It's over, and you know Mike, Mike Dukakis. Can't get a job mowing lawns, alright.* Crowd laughs. *I mean we just brutalize whoever loses and I know that."*

Romney's been defeated two times in his run for president and lost to Senator Ted Kennedy for Senate. After his loss to Kennedy in a senatorial campaign, he reportedly tells his brother, "I never want to run for something again unless I can win." Is it a competition, if the result is a forgone conclusion? Republicans seem to like rigged elections.

What did you think of Ronald Reagan's presidency? "Not much. Scott, look he was a nice guy. He didn't do much. Take a look at the Reagan years. Things did not change dramatically with his presidency. He was an interesting guy, but I never got a sense he was '*into'* politics very much."

Finally let's talk about the man who defeated you for president, George H.W. Bush. "He wasn't somebody I was particularly attracted to in terms of who he was and what he believed in politically. But I never had a feeling that Bush didn't have some strong moral conscience and had some principles."

You thought H.W. had integrity? "Yeah, I mean it wasn't my kind of integrity." If George Bush doesn't beat you there is no Supreme Court Justice Clarence Thomas, as he was a Bush appointee. "Oh my God, I still can't believe Thomas is in the Supreme Court."

"I remember when Bush announced his selection of Thomas. I said Jesus, I wouldn't have appointed Thomas for the District Court of Winchendon. That was one of my better lines," the fledgling comedian Duke said.

Governor, I feel like the public never got to know the humorous side of Michael Dukakis that I know. Would you agree with that? "Well, I didn't win the Presidency, so they never had a chance. Maybe that was my fault that I didn't show more of that side. Scott, I don't want to exaggerate this, but I'm often struck by the fact that the response to me on the street now is remarkably positive."

Governor, it's true, I've seen it many times. You're loved by so many people in Massachusetts and nationwide. "I'm not sure I ever perceived that. I'm quite often surprised by the feedback I get years later. Obviously, it makes me feel good."

It's candid moments like these that remind me of how honored I am to be present and recording this incredibly accomplished political heavyweight's final reflection of his life and career. As I was glancing at my notes for another question, Duke started talking unprompted. He had things he wanted to get off his mind.

"Having spent three terms in the office—and nobody has ever done it that long—and emerged with a good record. The guy who just left office, Baker, what was he doing with the T? It's terrible. Public transit system is the toughest job you have as governor."

Charlie Baker did not run for re-election as governor. He's currently the president of the NCAA. Baker brings out Duke's ire.

Do you think Baker was corrupt? "I don't think Charlie Baker is corrupt, but he's incompetent. I thought the guy who proceeded me, Francis Sargent, was reasonably competent. I didn't know he had a girlfriend," Duke says sheepishly.

Oh, OK, good to know. That's a jump in topics I didn't see coming. I'm not going to ask any follow-up questions because I really don't care about further details of Francis Sargent's (who passed away in 1998) love life or whom he may have lusted for.

Dukakis beat Sargent in 1974 to become Governor. One thing is perfectly clear as I spend more time with the Duke, he's not averse to gossip. "Scott, can I say a couple more things about Sargent and his girlfriend?" Sure. I'm going to the men's room but do continue on about Sargent. I can hear you...

The Iowa Chronicles

After graduating from American University in Washington, D.C. in 1987, I decided to head out to Hollywood to further my stand-up comedy career. My plan was to drive the cross-country trip from D.C. to Los Angeles.

My sister, Leslie, one of the ice cream servers ten years prior, was now an attorney in Washington D.C. She was a sought-after political lawyer in Federal Election Law. That was some magical ice cream.

She was hired to work for the Democratic Senator from Illinois, Paul Simon, as a lawyer to represent him for his bid for president. Simon was a pleasant, soft-spoken man who wore a bow tie and horn-rimmed glasses.

If you were looking to cast a guy running for president in 1887, Simon would be your man. He was a well loved senator, but was famous for sharing the name with, well of course, singer/songwriter, Paul Simon.

Once, I shared my Triple A TripTik itinerary with Leslie. she asked if I wanted to stop off in Iowa for a couple of weeks and work for the Simon campaign. She said it would be a chance to make some money along the way and get new comedy material. Good point.

I saw it as an opportunity to meet pretty girls who work on Democratic campaigns, as I went into comedy for the opportunity to sleep with waitresses. Hello, Des Moines.

The 1988 Democratic field for president was loaded with big names: Illinois Senator Paul Simon; Delaware Senator Joe Biden; Senator Al Gore from Tennessee; Jesse Jackson; Former Arizona Senator Bruce Babbitt; Missouri Congressman Dick Gephardt; former Colorado Senator Gary Hart, and Michael Dukakis.

Joe Biden dropped out in September of 1987 over the plagiarism of a speech scandal. All these years later, politicians haven't stopped plagiarizing speeches, they just stopped holding themselves accountable for the act. I wonder whatever happened to Biden?

Biden might have been stiff competition for the Duke. I really don't know what heinous act has to be committed in modern times to force a candidate to drop out of a race. Apparently, they could stand in the middle of Fifth Avenue, shoot somebody, and still not lose any voters.

I would depart D.C. with everything I owned in the back of my Suzuki Sidekick. You know you don't have a lot of life possessions when all your stuff is in the back seat of your car and it doesn't block your rearview mirror sightline.

The Suzuki Sidekick was shaped like a box. Any stiff wind while driving on a bridge and it was a 50/50 chance the Sidekick and I were going over the rails. I would be in Iowa or floating down a river by the New Year.

I drove into Des Moines on a dreary late December afternoon. I stopped in the downtown area and looked around for a couple of minutes. In a time of bewilderment on where my youthful path would lead me, a wave of calmness came upon me. I was finally sure of one thing: I knew that I would never live in Iowa.

I was given the role of canvassing for Simon in Des Moines. I would knock on residents' doors all day asking them to vote for Paul Simon, not the singer. Most people thought I was repping the Jehovah Witnesses or selling encyclopedias or vacuums cleaners, while all of them watched either Oprah or Phil Donahue. What I was amazed about was how friendly and giving Iowans were.

Sonny, would you like a drink or a fresh blueberry muffin out of the oven? Yes, both. *Did you want to come in and visit?* No, not at all.

Here, take this money for lunch or give this to Mr. Simon. Thank you. I'm keeping it. Never would consider otherwise.

I was raised in a blue-collar town in Massachusetts. You were brought up at a very young age to greet strangers at your door with the same line, "What the fuck do you want?" The politicians of today prey on these nice people for constant donations to line their pockets.

I was starting my second and final week hitting the pavement when I could see a group of canvassers heading toward me. You gotta be kidding! What! It's Governor Dukakis. That's my guy! This is awesome. Oh shit! I'm wearing a *Simon for President* t-shirt! I'm Benedict Freaking Arnold. Of all the gin joints and all the towns and all the nameless streets in all the world, Governor Dukakis walks down the one I'm on.

It's human nature to get excited when meeting anyone from your hometown area when you're traveling, and this was especially true in 1988. But this is the governor of my state who's currently running for President of the United States. I freaking know him.

Is my underwear showing? Is it still white? Do I have blueberries in my teeth? Smell under the armpits? I can't be wearing this shirt. Should I go up to him in the middle of an Iowa winter shirtless?

Of course, I would have chosen to work for Duke's campaign, if I was interested or had the opportunity to do such a thing. It's not that I wasn't going to vote for him for president or I was walking around wearing a Yankees hat, but at that moment, I sure looked and felt that way.

I turned my shirt inside out and walked up to the Duke. "Hello Governor, Scott Kerman from Methuen." *Hello, Scott, what are you doing here?* "Ahh, visiting some friends," I stammered. I don't know why a 21-year old man felt the need to lie, but that's what came out of my mouth.

It had been a few years since I saw him last, but he kicked into Uncle Mike instantly. *OK, Scott, make sure to volunteer when you get back home.* We shook hands and he headed off to the next house and on to a ham and bean supper in Dubuque. Or something like that.

Both Dukakis and I shouldn't have wasted our time, as Rep. Richard A. Gephardt from Missouri ended up narrowly defeating Simon in the Iowa Democratic presidential caucus and Duke finished in third place.

I ended up meeting a girl from the Gore campaign the following day and spending the night with her. The next morning, I woke up to find that my Sidekick had been broken into and all my clothes had been stolen. Are you freaking, freaking kidding me?

I headed out of town toward Los Angeles with only the clothes on my back. I was wearing a pair of jeans, my winter jacket, a Red Sox wool hat, and *Simon for President* t-shirt. I wore the shirt the duration of the trip. I can't tell you how many times, from Iowa to California, I heard someone ask, "Is Garfunkel his running mate?"

Years later, I was on a book tour and had an hour interview on a radio station from East Bum that clearly had needed lots of content filler. After awhile, it felt like a job interview. At one point, the radio host asked me if I could spend five minutes with anybody in the world, who would it be? I quickly replied, "The prick who stole all my stuff in Iowa."

Duke and Kitty's mailbox.

Dukakis door knocker.

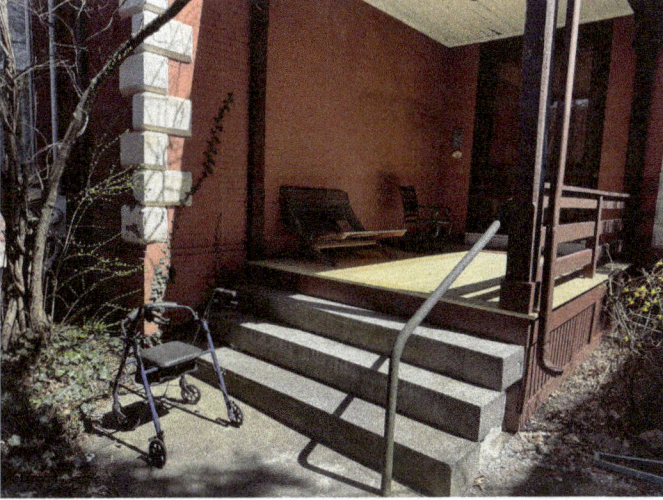

Infamous porch deck at Dukakis' house.

Duke greeting Scott at front door.

Duke and Scott at the kitchen table.

Duke looking over old photos.

Ambushed In Los Angeles

Scott, For some reason my emails don't seem to be transmitting. In any event, here is another try. We are wide open tomorrow. Can we get together then? Mike

"Scott, did you see my newspaper when you walked up the driveway? Where's my newspaper?" Duke is aggravated as his morning newspapers have not arrived and it's the middle of the afternoon. He gets the *Boston Globe* and *NY Times*.

The daily newspaper is dying a slow death. But not in the Dukakis household. He reads both papers front to back. A perk for many upon retirement or for people who work in a booth of some sort. I'm not a doctor, but it seems like this daily practice would keep your mind sharp at any age.

I write a weekly humor column for the Eagle Tribune newspaper in Massachusetts that covers Massachusetts and Southern New Hampshire. The paper was founded in 1868 and is still going strong. The readership is very loyal and a large percentage still receive the newspaper delivered.

I cancelled all my newspaper subscriptions in the past decade. Every day since I was three years old, I would wake up and get the morning *Boston Globe* sports page and sit on the throne. My father used to joke that I would never have learned how to read if it wasn't for the sports page. At least, I think he was joking.

The Sunday paper was a weekly, life-altering experience for many. Sometimes the paper seemed as heavy as a piano. Nothing could mess up a clean house more than the Sunday newspaper. Members of the household would each have their favorite sections. Everyone would go to their corners and start reading, and then meander over to grab more sections like they were checking out a book from the library.

If you told me I would ever spend a day without reading the sports page in my lifetime, I would have called you crazy. If you told me I would be writing a book with Governor Dukakis at the end of his life, I would have personally had you committed.

On this day, I want to discuss the infamous 1988 presidential debate with Dukakis and George Bush, Sr. Here comes Scott to rehash one of the most painful public moments of your life. You sure you want to answer the door?

As we sat down, I had made a last second decision. I wasn't going to play the video of the infamous debate question to the Duke. I would read it to him. That question is tough to watch and inappropriate in so many ways. It's absolutely cringe-worthy. Also, I didn't want Kitty to hear the audio from upstairs.

CNN anchor Bernard Shaw was moderating the second and final 1988 Presidential Debate with Dukakis vs. Bush in Los Angeles. Shaw welcomes the viewers, introduces his fellow panelists and quickly explains the rules. Shaw states there are no restrictions of what can be asked of the candidates.

Within 30 seconds of starting the debate program and saying Shaw and the panel could ask any question, no matter how horrific, Shaw moves in for the kill on Dukakis.

Governor, if Kitty Dukakis was raped and murdered would you favor an irrevocable death penalty for the killer?

In my mind, Shaw, who was a very respected journalist at the time, ambushed the Duke. Out of all the words in the English language at his disposal to ask such a question, Shaw felt the need to invoke the words, *rape, murder* and the Duke's wife's name. Not bad enough, Shaw had to create a scenario where Kitty was not only murdered, but raped for good measure. FYI, Kitty was seated in the front row.

Can you imagine talking to friends and your wife walks into the room and asks you what you're talking about? Oh, we were just speculating if you were raped and murdered, what penalty your murderer would receive.

Did you feel mentioning Kitty in the question was inappropriate? "I don't think it was wrong to do so. I did a bad job answering the question." Shaw could have said Jane Doe. "Yes, he could have," said Duke. "But I should have knocked that question out of the ballpark."

Dukakis' answer was described as a candidate's career-killer and changed the trajectory of the race. Unprofessional journalism at the very least and suspicious intentions could be inferred. Shaw died in 2022 at the age of 82. In his obituary, the question was included as one of the highlights of his career. I'd call it a lowlight. If it was revealed someday that the question was planted by the Bush camp, I wouldn't be shocked. This has Bush's campaign manager Lee Atwater's DNA all over it.

The first word in answering the question that came out of Dukakis' mouth for the biggest night of his life was *"No."* Not a great way to start any conversation in the history of communication, much less a presidential debate. Especially when the country is watching to choose who will run the United States of America and influence the free world.

"And I think you know I opposed the death penalty during all of my life," Dukakis says emotionless.

Yeah, people watching had already stopped listening to him by that second sentence of the night. I think I've decided on who I'm going to vote for president. Time for dessert and maybe catch the last of the Cosby Show.

On June 27,1988, Mike Tyson beat Michael Spinks in a much-hyped, heavyweight-championship boxing match. Tyson knocked Spinks out in ninety-one seconds. In two blinks of an eye, the fight was over. If you went to the bathroom, you missed it. Less than four months later, on October 13, the presidential debate was over in less than a blink of the other eye.

Dukakis always takes the high road. Add this trait to the lengthy list of reasons why I admire him. "It was a perfectly legitimate question. I had a problem on how I dealt with the issue."

"I should have said what was going on in Houston with the death penalty compared to what was going on in Massachusetts. I think I should have said it repeatedly and forcefully, that the death penalty is not a deterrent."

If you had answered the question in that way, do you believe it would have been a game changer? "Yes, I believe so." Did you and your staff think you were going to be asked a question about the death penalty? "Oh yeah." Did you have practice debates? "Yes." But you didn't practice that type of death penalty question? Duke shakes his head and rubs his hands together.

I think he was in a no-win situation. If he answered with personal feelings concerning the fictional raping and murder of his wife, he would appear to be waffling on his strong stand against the death penalty. Answer it straight up with no emotions and you seem non-caring toward your beloved wife's imaginary plight.

Why do you feel so strongly against the death penalty? "I don't want to kill people. Let them spend the rest of their life in jail." That's it? "That's enough. Scott, what do you think?" He asks. Governor, I'm against the death penalty. I think the criminal justice system can be corrupted and innocent people get executed.

My father, who was a lawyer, always quoted Benjamin Franklin, *"It's better 100 guilty persons should escape than one innocent person suffer."* Duke nods in approval.

I wanted very badly to be animated and rip into Shaw's way of asking the death penalty question and throw out accusations about

George H.W. Bush and his merry men. But I've learned I have to refrain from raising my voice with emotion and must keep an even keel or Duke will shut down.

I once interviewed NFL Hall of Fame offensive lineman, John Hannah, who played for the New England Patriots, for a feature story. We got along quite well and talked a number of times in person and on the phone. Hannah is a very large man from Alabama and a great guy. I brought up the Patriots vs Oakland Raiders AFC divisional round playoff game in 1976. This game would go down as one of the most disputed contests in NFL history. I guess I have a sick habit of bringing up people's worst career moments.

The Patriots were an exciting young team who were playing the John Madden coached Raiders. With the Patriots leading 21-17 nearing the end of the fourth quarter, Raiders quarterback, Ken Stabler, threw an incomplete pass to give the Patriots an inevitable victory. But wait, what the hell is that? A late penalty flag is on the field. Referee Ben Dreith called a phantom 'roughing-the-passer' call on Patriots defensive lineman Sugar Bear Hamilton, who had tipped Stabler's pass. This gave the Raiders a first down and, ultimately, the victory. The Raiders went on to win the Super Bowl. This was the only time Madden would win a Super Bowl title as a head coach.

I was ten years old and a huge Patriots fan. After that game, I cried for a month straight. This was one of my first life lessons that people suck, especially sports referees. Despite the Patriots six Super Bowl victories since, I'm still pissed off about that game.

If the Patriots won that game, they would have surely gone on to win the Super Bowl, guaranteeing my childhood would have been relatively angst free. John Madden would have been just another guy and there are no Madden video games. Kids would have gone outside and played more. We would never have had childhood obesity, a de-emphasis on education, or Trump. Just generations of happy, healthy, well-adjusted, Adderall-free kids. Or something like that.

If Duke had become president, there isn't a George H.W. Bush presidency or one for his son George W. There's no Clarence Thomas on the Supreme Court. 9/11 might not have happened and there's no invasion of Iraq and Afghanistan, to name a few. No dogs would ever die and people would always be honest and kind to each other. Or something like that.

"Scott, I played in the game and you're angrier than I am about what happened," said Hannah. This is how I feel concerning the Shaw debate question debauchery. I've never liked the name Ben since that fateful game. I'll add the name Bernard to the mix.

It All Ends Up Worth a Nickel

Scott, I am still recovering from my illness and have to see doctors next week. I'll get back to you after I finish those visits. Mike

My wife and I are yard sale junkies. Every Saturday morning in the summer, we head out yard-saling. New England is a hot bed of hidden treasures well preserved in countless cluttered attics. If you need a sea captain lamp, just call me, I've got plenty of them.

On one particular Saturday, I was looking around a garage full of stuff and there was a table of assorted trinkets. I noticed three *Dukakis/Bentsen* pins from the 1988 DNC convention on the table. The first one had a simple outline of the map of the United States with *Dukakis and Bentsen 1988* printed inside it. The second pin had another outline of a highway billboard with lights on top with *Dukakis and Bentsen and 1988*. Both pins looked like they were created using an Etch-a-Sketch. It appears the *Dukakis/Bentsen* campaign was running for eighth-grade student council.

The third pin was in blue lettering and actually had some depth in the color. It read simply *Mike Dukakis*. It was pinned to a thin purple ribbon that read *Dukakis Delegate* that was the same type of ribbon you received as a prize in the 1980s for finishing in second place in a kids' wheelbarrow race.

The office supply store chain, Staples, opened its first store in 1986 in the Brighton neighborhood of Boston a couple of miles from Duke's house. Knowing him as I do, and how he combines frugality with micro-managing, I would suspect he personally got a great bulk deal from Staples to make those pins and ribbons. It sure looked like it. For reference, the *Bush/Quayle* pins were a colorful red, white, blue and gold, and each candidate's photo was pictured in their very own star. George Bush's picture is bright and happy, with Bush giving a big toothy smile. Dan Quayle's picture is dark, and he appears unshaven. Quayle has a serious look, as if he's starring as a private detective in a 1970s television crime drama. *Quayle always gets his man! Tuesday nights at 9pm on CBS.*

I picked up the three pins and went up to a middle-aged female running the sale. I first negotiated the price of an Abbott and Costello comic book I had picked up priced at three dollars. I smoothly got her down to one dollar. I then showed her the three Dukakis pins. "Oh, those have sentimental value," she said. She wanted five dollars total for the three pins. It seems like sentimentality used to be worth more.

She said her mother was a Dukakis delegate at the convention. I told her I was working on a book project with the Dukakis and she screamed, "He's still alive? I thought he was dead!" No, he's very much alive. "Well, tell him Anne from Massachusetts says hello." OK, I sure will.

I got her down to three dollars for the pins. It's physically impossible for me to pay full price at a yard sale. This chapter may never had been written if Anne didn't go down two dollars in price.

As we were leaving the sale, Anne screamed, "You're not bull-shitting me are you?" What, about me writing a book with Governor Dukakis? "No, that he's still alive. Are you sure?"

On my next visit to see the very much alive Governor, the first thing I noticed is that I didn't hear the dog barking. Where's the dog? "Scott, the dog was a pain in the ass. Kitty loved her. Kind of. We gave the dog away to a good home. The dog is gone and I'm not mourning its departure." We both laughed.

Governor, can a woman be elected president? "Yes," he answers. He starts speaking in glowing terms about the current governor of Massachusetts, Maura Healey, the first female elected to the office. "Can't argue that she's not capable, an interesting gal," he says with a smile.

Of course, calling a female a *gal* publicly has gone away with his generation. One of the most famous liberals in the last half century would have been eaten by his own kind for using a word like that. Duke isn't any less a liberal, it's just the line has moved far left from his sight.

Since John F. Kennedy was elected president in 1960, there have been three former public servants from Massachusetts to become the nominees of their party: Michael Dukakis, John Kerry, and Mitt Romney. All of them were defeated in the general election. Can a politician from Massachusetts ever become president again? "I think so, I hope so," says Duke.

Did being from Massachusetts help or hurt you? "I think a lot of it has to do with what happens during the campaign." You had a big lead at one point? "Allegedly. All this polling. Polls weren't solid. I'm skeptical. A whole campaign is ahead of you and the first thing that happens is polls. Let's count the votes."

The home phone rings and Duke starts talking to a telemarketer. He begins asking the person questions about what he's selling. Duke has the ability to take control of any conversation he's involved in and make you glad to come for the ride.

The person on the other end is not just another annoyance to him, it's a person trying to make a living. It's a person he tried so hard in political office to serve in their best interest. Also, for three decades in his life, they were a potential vote. Duke tells the person he needs to go and wishes him good luck in the future.

You receive a lot of calls from telemarketers and strangers, don't you? "I do. Scott, it could be because our phone number's in the phone book." There's two words I haven't heard in well over a decade. Governor, do you have a phone book? "Of course. Who doesn't?" Ahh, hardly anyone else. "I just had a Greek guy call me who's in town visiting from Wichita who wanted to come over and take a picture with me." What? Oh gosh. Governor, lets not do that. "OK."

Can you imagine this Massachusetts Tourism Bureau marketing campaign?

Come to Massachusetts and visit such famous places as Fenway Park, Faneuil Hall Marketplace and the Museum of Fine Arts. Take an historic morning walk along the Freedom Trail and, after lunch in the North End, drive over to former Governor Michael Dukakis' house to take pictures with him. Note: Please, call him first before going over.

"Scott, not to get off the subject, but I've been reading the Stephen Kinzer book on the two Dulles brothers," he says. An avid reader, Duke carefully chooses his next book to read by reading whatever book is handed to him next.

"Secretary of State John Foster Dulles and Allen Dulles, who was the head of the CIA, served both at the same time when Eisenhower was president. But they were quite different." How so? "John Foster was much more sober, much more faithful to his wife. Unlike his brother Allen, who was a notorious womanizer. Scott, how the hell did he get away with it? I have no idea. I can't figure it out. In this day and age, I don't think it would have worked. Do you?"

Huh, I've never really thought about it until this very second. OK, I do not think it would work today with iPhones and social media. Shockingly, I had no follow-up questions on the Dulles boys or how to cheat on your wife successfully. Governor, thank you for sharing.

A few days earlier, I had returned home from New York with my wife where we visited my 92-year-old uncle, Noah, and his lovely wife, Eva. I enjoy sitting with Noah at the kitchen table and talking, just like I do with Duke. Noah's a very distinguished, brilliant man who remains as sharp as a tack. He was born and raised in Russia and moved to the U.S. to practice medicine over 60 years ago. Both the Duke and Noah were extremely successful in their fields of endeavor, but very different in their backgrounds and professions.

Noah jumps into a new story in a very similar way as the Duke. We were talking about heated gloves and next thing you know, "Scott, you have to realize doctors and nurses would work very long hours at times and that one can't always control the power of the flesh." Right. There are three heat controls…

In a 48-hour period, I had two older men in my life, whom I cherish, choose to share with me their random thoughts on infidelity completely unsolicited. I've come to realize that the Silent Generation seems to have plenty to say.

Campaign pins from Duke's presidential bid.

Can I Get a Bus Transfer?

It was another cold, wintry day in Brookline, Mass. where it would snow, sleet, rain and turn to ice, all in an hour's time. In New England, we call this a Tuesday. The doorbell rang and it was 'Uncle Joe' the mailman. Joe's my great friend and one of the smartest people I've ever met. He's a real-life Cliff Clavin character, but Joe actually does know it all.

Joe came into the house to warm up and talk Boston sports. "It's weather like this that's going to make me retire," groused Joe, who's in his mid-sixties. He logs over 20,000 steps per day walking his route in all kinds of weather. Postal workers are an under-appreciated group.

I poured him a cup of coffee and we sat down. "I just saw Duke and Kitty," he said. Joe's the Duke's mailman. Joe likes to ring their doorbell to give them their mail or a package to make sure they receive it, and to have an excuse to see them. They always invite him in.

"What were they up to?" I said. Joe began shaking his head. "They were waiting at the bus stop to go downtown for Kitty's doctor's appointment," he said. "You have to be kidding," I said, worried. "No, I offered to punch out and drive them, but you know the Duke," Joe said.

"So, what you're telling me is that an eighty-plus-year-old couple is standing outside in a storm where even the lamp posts are looking for cover?" I exclaimed. Joe nodded, as he took off his winter hat that had ice particles on it. "We had a nice talk. They were quite happy," he said.

Joe and I discussed the Patriots for awhile and he stood up to go back out into the storm to continue his route. The sound of sleet pelting the kitchen window was distracting. "Joe, if Duke and Kitty are still out outside, they're probably frozen into statues," I said. Joe laughed. "That'd be the only way he'd ever let them build a statue of him." I opened the door for Joe and the storm wanted inside. "The Duke frozen at a T bus stop with Kitty at his side until the end of time. I think he'd like that," Joe said as he put his hat on, bent his head and disappeared into the winter abyss.

Thankfully, the Dukakis' survived their venture into the teeth of the winter nor'easter storm. Duke thawed out enough to let me in the house for my next visit.

"Scott, were you here when I went through the porch?" He asked it so matter-of-factly, as if he was mentioning he had potato chips with his sandwich. No, I was not here. What happened?

"I fell through the porch." I didn't hear about this. "Well, I've recovered quite quickly. One leg down, one leg up. I haven't gotten back fully, so maybe that's a sign of age." No, it would be a sign that the ground under you collapsed.

I'm pretty sure the broken porch flooring should have been addressed long before the Duke went through it. If he had become president, he would still have had a Secret Service detail. Maybe they could have brought some nails and wood with them to work. Another negative to not becoming president. The hits never end.

Governor, when you've watched presidents speak over the years since the 1988 election, do you ever think you should have been in that position? "No, I had my chance and didn't win."

If I had lost an election to be president, there would never be a food I would bite into that didn't taste bitter.

Was there a time in your life that you lacked confidence? "Yes, when Ed King beat me for re-election as governor." You lost the Democratic primary as the incumbent in 1978 to King? "Yeah, Jesus," Duke says in disgust. "I knew one thing that happens when you get in politics is that you might lose an election. But I was up eighteen points in the polls over King with one month to go and lost."

How's that possible? Did they have second graders doing the polling? "I don't know what it was. It's not that I was taking it lightly, but just about everybody else was taking it lightly. Though I was much more concerned than other people. I couldn't be beaten and so on and so forth."

On election day, did you think you were in trouble? "No, I don't think so, not really." It was that much of a shock? "Well, you're ready for anything in this business. Next thing I know, I lose by around seven or eight points, and nobody expected that including myself. I didn't expect to lose, and I lost. All I can tell you is, it was not fun."

So, if we're to believe the pollsters, in one month's time, twenty-five percent of the voters changed their mind and voted against the incumbent?

Governor, I don't understand what happened? "Me neither. It was a very disappointing result and after the election, I really didn't think I had a future in politics." At that time that had to be the most humbling moment of your political career. "I've had a lot of humbling moments," Duke laughs. At that time? "Sure."

Your head must have been spinning? "At first, I said to myself you better go back to being a lawyer or something. But all kinds of people came up to me and said this is terrible you should run again. But then people started reacting to the fact that King was going to be governor. As I slowly recovered," Duke laughs.

I read where Kitty called losing that election a 'public death'. "Is that what she called it?" Yes. "It was bad. It didn't last long fortunately." I can totally picture Kitty saying it. "Yeah".

Why do you think you lost the King election? "Just a certain amount of complacency. Tough to get people stirred up when you have an 18-point lead. After the election, I thought to myself you lost, that was going to be the end of politics for me. Then I thought King was King and I was me."

A loss like that would have had some guys growing a beard, moving to Tibet, and opening a mutton stand. Duke laughs, "Scott, I spent a lot of time thinking about it before I got back into it. Woulda.. shoulda… You have to keep moving forward."

"After some months, I came back and got back into it with a lot of support and won again. And did a much better job my second term, because I didn't take it for granted. I was never complacent again."

So, when you had a 17-point lead in the polls against Bush did you think of the King defeat? "Yes, I knew the poll was meaningless." So much for polls. "But I made one serious mistake." In the presidential election? "Yes, and you know what that is."

It haunts Duke more than ever. I just call it the Houston thing at this point. He mentions it at least once per visit. "Bush's hometown had a murder rate of six times that of Boston. They had the death penalty, we didn't. How's it a deterrent to violent crime?" You're right. "Bush started coming at me and I should have said, 'Hey, look at your town and look at mine, what do you prefer?'"

Did you enjoy being a public person? "All depends on how you're doing. But yes, it put me in a position to make some important decisions that I hope affected people in a positive way. If you don't enjoy making public policy that makes a difference in the lives of people, then find something else to do."

Does a politician have to have a strong ego? "Did I take a lot of personal satisfaction that I was able to make a difference in people's lives? Sure. That's why you do it. Are you able to handle public exposure and the criticism that comes from time to time? If you can't handle it, you're in the wrong business."

When you ran for governor, I assume you had a plan if you were elected? "Yeah, do things. Bring people together. Get things done. Pick excellent people, which is so important. It's a great job. Being governor of Massachusetts has to be the best job in the world. Just remarkable."

This is what I don't get, Governor. You have your dream job. Governor of Massachusetts. You're good at it. You live in your hometown. You have a wonderful family and close friends. Why did you run for president? Duke pauses for a moment. "Scott, because I felt there were even more important things to do."

Seemingly at least once during my visit, Duke will receive a call from a former student wanting to share with him what's going on with them and get his advice. On this day, the phone rings and Duke is able to pick it up and answer the call before the answering machine gets it. Duke wins! He's like Yoda from Star Wars. Small in size, but wise, and willing to share his knowledge.

He hangs up and begins filling a glass of water for me from the sink and turns to me quickly. "Scott, this may sound strange to you, but campaigning is grueling and boring. Saying the same goddamn thing day after day and making it different is difficult."

I was taken aback by how brutally honest and comfortable he has become with me. Not that "damn" is even considered a swear word anymore, but this was emotion I enjoyed seeing from him. These kitchen visits have proved perfect for peeling back the onion.

You have said you enjoyed being governor because you had the ability to help people. "Particularly to walk into a political situation that was in desperate shape and to do some significant things that made life better for people. There's no question Massachusetts is a better state now than when I arrived. There's no comparison."

The Duke is right. In a new study by WalletHub, Massachusetts once again took home the gold as the "best state to live in in 2023."

The two studies ranked on similar factors such as affordability, economy, safety, quality of life, health and education.

Kitty calls for Duke from the top of the stairs. I've been married for 27 years, I'm quite familiar with that tone. Despite both of us wanting to continue our visit, it's an appropriate time to end it for the day. As Duke walks me out, I wave to Kitty.

"When are you coming back?" I've been trying to visit every two weeks like clockwork, but it seems he would like it to be sooner. How's next week sound? He smiles. "Sounds good, call me early next week and we will figure out a time." OK.

I give the Duke a hug and I'm on my way. As I get home, my wife is waiting at the top of the stairs for me. Fun time is over for both of us on this day.

Turkey Soup For You And You

As usual, Duke answers the door all smiles. We sit down in the kitchen and I notice he's black and blue under both of his eyes. Otherwise, he sounds good and is walking around quite well. There's a youthful exuberance to Duke that never waivers, despite his body not cooperating at times.

I'm 58 and wake up each morning taking inventory on what aches more than when I went to sleep. Sometimes the biggest question of my day is if my new pain is a muscle pull or a bone bruise? I can't imagine what can happens to your body overnight when you're 90.

Let's talk about the legend of your Thanksgiving turkey soup. "That was just an accident." So, you had friends and family bring over their leftover Thanksgiving turkey carcasses for soup, is that right? "Yes, someone brought me over a half of a turkey, which got me started on making the soup, and then more people started doing it." You freeze them to make turkey soup? "That's right."

The Boston Globe found this out and did an article on it? "Yes, they did it a while back." In 2015, the *Globe* interviewed Dukakis for a Thanksgiving piece on his turkey carcass collection. He was then interviewed on CNN on Thanksgiving day and the story went viral the next day, Black Friday. CNN said the resulting Dukakis/turkey carcass frenzy sent Twitter into a tailspin.

"I started having turkey carcasses showing up at my front door. First about eight or nine of them showed up, then there was more than that, and then more than that! I think the total was 29. Finally, we gotta stop. This is crazy!" Were they just leaving it at the front door or ringing the doorbell? "Most rang the doorbell and put them on the porch and left."

Leaving the dead remains of a bird on the doorstep of a former governor and presidential candidate is usually what constitutes the opening scene of a political thriller movie. "I made a lot of turkey soup with them and I gave about half of them away. I couldn't keep up with them all. Throwing out a turkey carcass is *terrible*!"

Can you imagine that phone call? "Hello, this is Governor Michael Dukakis." The person on the other line might be thinking this could be the moment that changes their life forever. How can I help you, Governor? "Do you want a leftover turkey carcass?" Huh?

I love how passionate Duke is about things big and small. It all matters. However, I'm thinking the word *terrible* should be saved for more important issues than the preserving of turkey bones. Maybe it's just me.

Do you have a special recipe for turkey soup? "My mother's." Do you have it written down? I figured it would be on a card somewhere with his mother's handwriting. "I think so, I'll see if I can find it. I may have it somewhere. I'll do my best." I'm not inclined to give a 90-year-old man a homework assignment, so I'm not going to hold my breath. What's the recipe?

"Tossing in the rest of the bird, onion, carrots, rice, some pasta usually, vegetables if they were hanging around, pepper, salt. Nothing fancy. Scott, I was eating or drinking turkey soup my whole life. I loved it from the time I was three or four years old. I was making it myself by the time I was six years old. It was my favorite meal. It's good for you and it lasts. Very important, it's cheap," Duke laughs. "All of those good things." *This paragraph was sponsored by the Great Depression.*

Do you still cook? "Not for the last year or so. My son John cooks my dinner. I cooked a good deal." What were your favorite dishes to cook? "I cooked everything." Greek food? "Yes. I kept doing it until one of my legs hit below surface." He can't go long without a mention of the aging porch deck incident or Trump. One of them is going to be the death of us all.

Are you using a walker at times when you walk? "I use my cane and that seems to work well. At some point, I suppose I'm going to have to use that rolling thing." He means the walker. He likes it as much as he likes dogs, Charlie Baker and Trump.

The walker sitting on the porch, is that Kitty's? "I think John basically got that for me. I'm trying to use the cane, but at some point, I may have to use that thing. So here we are."

Note. The walker—and henceforth, Trump—is only described by Duke using the adjective "that" so as not to fully recognize its existence.

"I've had an awful good life, no question about it." Do you have any regrets in your political life other than the presidential campaign? "No, I don't think so. But that loss is a big regret."

You were in the Army stationed in Korea. "Yes, after the Korean War. I was in a unit very close to the DMZ and I was there for 16 months until I came back to the states." Duke was in the Army from 1955-57 as a radio operator.

"I became fairly fluent in Korean. I wanted to learn the language, but if you don't use it on a daily basis you won't retain it for long. I didn't have much of an opportunity to practice it."

Duke starts speaking in Korean. He looks at me like I have a clue about what he's saying. After he stops, I don't know if I should react by laughing, crying or nodding my head. I look down under his chin for subtitles. Nothing. I have to give him some feedback. Governor, it sounds like Korean to me. He smiles.

Are you fluent in Spanish? "Yes, until a few years ago." You spoke some Spanish during your nomination speech. "That's right, I enjoy it." Do you realize how cutting edge that would have been to have a president in 1988 who was bilingual? "Si." Here we go. Duke starts speaking Spanish. I can understand a few words, but not much. He has a big smile on his face. After going on for a minute, he asks me, in English, "What did I just say?" I reply, *No se*. Which means I don't know. "That's very good." Duke just complimented me for knowing nothing. I love this guy! "I forgot what I just said," Duke chuckles while saying it. We both belly-laugh. I can testify that we were sober during the entire discussion of foreign languages, it just may not sound that way.

I took four years of Spanish in high school. They didn't know how to teach foreign languages back then. It was just lots of vocabulary words. I never learned how to converse. Though, if you need to know how to say the number *35* in broken Spanish, you can call me.

"Scott, Greek and Spanish accents are quite similar. It was quite easy to do Spanish and sound virtually like a native. People would come up to me or I would go up to people and start talking Spanish. They would say, 'Jesus, where did this guy come from?'" I think many Republicans have said the same thing.

I can see a glint in your eye when you're speaking Spanish, you really enjoy it. "Very much so. Any opportunity, I'll speak it." He reminds me of my cousin who loves to juggle. If he sees any of the same items in threes or more, he'll start juggling them. Balls, cans, pens, utensils, you name it. Though, he can't seem to juggle his finances as he's filed for bankruptcy three times.

How many languages do you speak? "I speak English, Greek Spanish, Korean so-so." Growing up you spoke Greek and English in the house? "Yes, and I had my grandparents living with us and they spoke very little English. When I spoke to them or my relatives it was in Greek, not English." Did speaking Spanish help you as governor? "Most definitely."

Did being a military veteran help you in running for political office? "Yep, it's part of who I was." Did you take advantage of the GI bill? "I don't think it was offered. I certainly would have had I the opportunity to do so." The original GI bill expired in 1956. "It did?" You should have gotten in on that. "You're right." You can see Duke thinking he missed out on some dough he was entitled to. Somebody in the federal government might be getting a call tomorrow.

Governor, my father said the GI bill changed his life. He fought in the Army in World War II and took advantage of the GI bill to go to undergraduate and law school. He said the U.S. government paid him more on a monthly basis when was going to school than when he was a soldier. "That doesn't surprise me. What an important bill." After hearing that story, he'll probably make that call as soon as I leave.

Apparently, the Democrats have weak support right now with the Latino vote. Why is that? "Cause they're dealing with Spanish speakers and non-Spanish speakers and it's a complicated thing. Why would they be attracted to Trump at all?" Duke slipped up and said his name. "Why is anybody attracted to That Guy. I don't understand it."

When push comes to shove, do Latinos tend to be conservative? "Yeah, they do. Look, within one generation they're speaking English—speaking Spanish as well—but also speaking English.

A lot of them are conservative because they're business people. It's the American system."

I begin wrapping it up for the day and take a very nice picture of Duke standing at the table. "Scott, look what happens. That Guy is what, the third generation now? I don't know what he is." Somehow, we've made a sharp turn back to That Guy. "His grandfather was German, great grandfather. I don't know and he's a shit!" It took Trump to evoke the first harder-core curse word from Duke in all my time with him. He's graduated from 'damn'. I'm surprised Duke didn't say the Spanish word for shit, *mierda'.* There's always the next visit.

We've Got a Visitor

I've had Red Sox season tickets at Fenway Park since 2003. Until 2020, I was located in section 8 of the grandstands, which inspired the name of my show, The Grandstanders. The seats are the best deal in the ballpark. I call section 8 the affordable housing program of the Boston Red Sox. It's located in right field and the seats point toward right field. They force you to turn to look at home plate. Welcome to the Fenway Park experience! The ballpark was built in 1912, so I guess back then people had more flexible necks.

Four years ago, I relocated to section 30 in the grandstands, where you can see home plate without needing a chiropractor. The group that sits next to me are writers from *The Boston Globe* who share season tickets. This is how I met retired *Globe* writer, Steven Kurkjian, 80, who has received three Pulitzer Prizes for his investigative reporting. Kurkjian covered Dukakis during his days as governor and when I mentioned him to Duke, he said how he always liked and respected him.

Governor, do you want me to see if Stephen can join us next time? "I would like that very, very much," Duke replied enthusiastically. Done deal.

"It's so good to see you, my friend," greets Dukakis to Kurkjian as they meet in the front hall of the Dukakis home. We all sit down at the dining room table. Duke's energy is sky high and his excitement is palpable. These two older, highly-accomplished men start talking a mile a minute like friends on a playground, rapidly moving from topic to topic—The Vietnam War, LBJ, Greek and Armenian cultures, Strom Thurmond, how Bates College compares to Swarthmore College—I can't keep track.

These two guys from the Silent Generation are not living up to that reputation. Neither seem to take a breath. I call it after five minutes: This was a really good idea.

"As you know, I'm against term limits," says Duke. I don't even know how that subject came up. Kurkjian starts yelling and clapping, "Go for it! Go for it! We'll have you in front of the parade again!" I feel like I should be waving a rally towel.

Governor, why are you against term limits? "If Ted Kennedy is a good legislator and will be a good one for 40 years, why should he not be able to continue to serve if elected?" He replies. "Yes, Yes, Yes!" Kurkjian agrees exuberantly. Now I feel like I'm at a church revival.

Kurkjian asks Dukakis if he can call his cousin Rick Gureghian, who worked for Dukakis in the press office, and have him join in. Rick lives in Las Vegas and is in poor health. Rick's girlfriend, Lee Ann, answers the phone and says she took two of Dukakis' master's courses at Northeastern. "I hope I did well," says the Duke. "You did great," she responds.

Good luck finding someone in Massachusetts over 50 years old who doesn't have some connection with Dukakis. Rick did not know Stephen was calling with Dukakis in tow. "Rick, I have a friend who's sitting next to me who remembers you with such great fondness, Governor Michael Dukakis," Stephen says so eloquently.

"Are you kidding? Hello, Governor," says Gureghian. "Rick, how are you, my friend?" Rick begins to cry uncontrollably. It makes my own tears threaten. Hold on, Dukakis and Stephen have dry eyes, I need to keep it together. "Great to hear your voice, I miss working for you, Governor," says an emotional Gureghian.

Rick proceeds to tell a story about how he set up a State House meeting with Dukakis and Mick Jagger of *The Rolling Stones* in 1989. *The Rolling Stones* were playing at Sullivan Stadium for their *Steel Wheels* tour. Jagger said he would be honored to meet the governor and that he was a big fan. How long ago was this? Well, it was bass guitarist Bill Wyman's last tour, so it was a week before Ron Wood joined the band.

The week prior to Kurkjian's visit, *The Rolling Stones* performed at Gillette Stadium. Maybe it's not too late for Duke to be in front of the parade again.

Governor, when you were elected, you came in and tackled corruption, as well as nepotism. "Patronage was a way of life. If you wanted a job, you had to know somebody," says Duke. "The wink and the nod was a way of life back then."

"You stopped that. You said, 'no way," says Kurkjian. "Prior administrations had somebody whom they knew or were related to and they were in jobs all over. They weren't terrible people or crooks, they just didn't do anything in their jobs," Duke says. We all laugh. "By the end of my first month in office, that stuff was over. I said what!" says Duke. "The word was out that this guy's different," adds Kurkjian.

"Governor, how rampant were no-show jobs when you took office?" I asked. "It was all over the state. They were straight out stealing. I put an end to that in my first 30 days." "Yes, you did, sir. Yes, indeed," said Kurkjian.

How do you think *The Boston Globe* treated you overall as governor? "Fine. Guys like Stephen and others didn't get much wrong." Responsible journalism, what a unique concept. "The different thing about Michael Dukakis was that he had the intellectual prowess to convince you in an argument that his policy was a better policy. He drove home that first term; honesty in government with full disclosure. Conflicts of interest were no longer going to be allowed," said Kurkjian, as Duke smiles in approval.

Duke and Kurkjian dig into a Greek tapioca pudding cup that Kurkjian brought for the two of them, along with a box of pastries. I dive into some Tiramisu. There is no reason for any of us to get up from this table anytime for the next month.

Governor, full transparency was very important to you? "Yes, at all times," Duke strongly replies. "He put together a state ethics commission where you had every political figure from state reps to governor having to fill out a disclosure form. What did you own? What did your family own? Were there any state contracts in your holdings? This put people on notice," says Kurkjian.

Governor, how important was Kurkjian and the Spotlight Team of the *Globe*? This was a special reporting unit within the newspaper for investigative journalism and accountability. "They set the stage for a tough, feared journalistic initiative. It wasn't just once. As soon as they would be finished with one, they would be onto the next one," says Duke.

"Thank you, Governor. You knew you hit it on the nose when you got a call from him or his office saying, 'Send me a summary of that, with the names, and we'll be acting on it,'" says Kurkjian.

Governor, do investigative reporters like Kurkjian keep the community on their toes with the idea that if you mess up, a guy like him could be walking through the door and you're going to be held accountable? "I don't think there is any question."

"It's not like we're tough guys or anything. We used the resources that the governor put in place as a legislator and as governor," says Kurkjian. "I think the governor took advantage of the times when change was in the air. His intelligence, his directness, his insistence on honesty. This is how we're going to run an administration. We needed a fresh approach to politics, and he changed the way things worked in state politics. You made progressivism the standard," says Kurkjian. "I think so, and we never looked back," says Duke.

Stephen, how important was it for the governor to have presided over a period of such economic growth for Massachusetts in the eighties? Steve and I exclaim at the same time, "The Massachusetts Miracle!" "This state thrives economically today because of the foundation the governor laid down," says Kurkjian. Duke smiles ear to ear.

Stephen, has there ever been a better advocate for public service than Governor Dukakis? "That's an accurate assertion. He was the best advocate. He brought in the best and the brightest. Because if you had the brains and the voice, you could make a difference. You saw it in him." says an animated Kurkjian.

This has been such a fantastic visit. "Blessed memories," says Kurkjian. "You're great to put us together." "We did a lot of good stuff together," says Duke. "We did! We did!" Kurkjian agrees.

"Governor, have you gotten over to Fenway Park this year," asks Kurkjian. Duke replies, "As much as I could." Which is none, I'm laughing to myself. What a seasoned-politician answer. "Governor, Scott goes to more Red Sox games than some of the players," Kurkjian jokes. We all start laughing, still buried in our desserts.

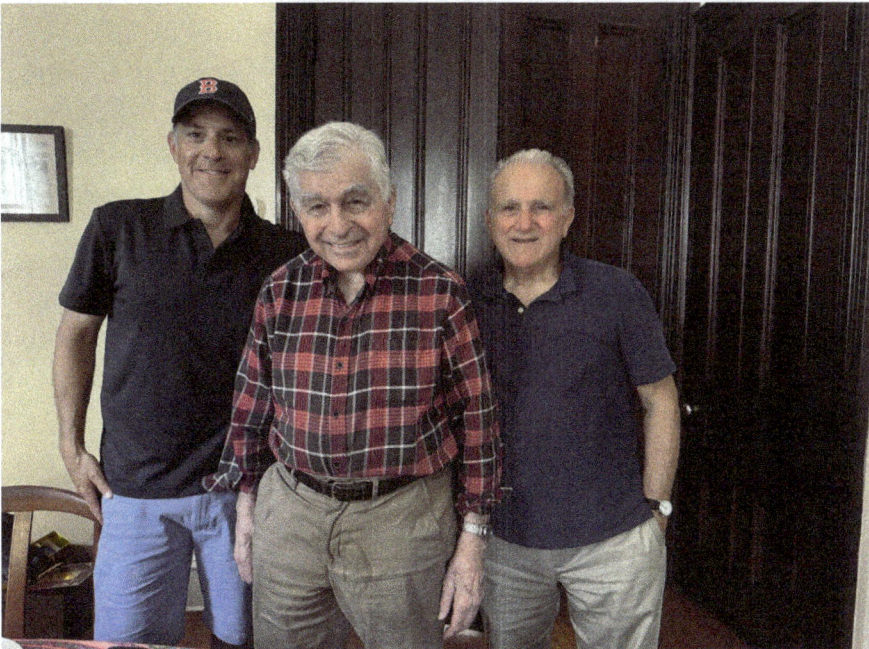

Duke, Scott and Boston Globe's Stephen Kurkjian

Duke and Kitty Forever

Email: *Governor, I hope Kitty is feeling better real soon.*

Duke*: Me, too, but she is in a lot of pain, I'll keep you posted.*

I had not come to the house for three weeks as Duke hasn't been feeling well. As Duke greets me at the door, he immediately mentions how he has self-diagnosed a *charley horse*. A charley horse is a muscle spasm in the leg. If I ever reach the Duke's age, I'm sure I'll be a walking muscle spasm.

"I don't know how I got this darn thing," says a frustrated Duke. He has been an active, daily walker his whole life. His life's steps would probably blow up a FitBit. I don't try to theorize what might have caused his injury; my non-professional answer is that he's really old. Both charley and his horse. The average life expectancy of a U.S. male is 73 years old. Duke's got that by 17 years and counting. He acts like he's a professional athlete who's been put on the injured list. He comes across as a person much younger than his age. Mind over body. When he dies, he'll no doubt be the most surprised person in the room.

He walks gingerly as he brings me into the living room, tugging at the back of his leg as we sit on the couch. "This is more comfortable for me," he says. A move from the kitchen table to the couch. I've graduated to the adult table. I still prefer the kitchen.

How's Kitty's condition? "Gradually getting better. But it's long and slow." How much of a toll is it taking on you? "I spend most of my time and day with her and next to her. I do my walk and occasionally go out to events and that kind of thing. Kitty sleeps a lot."

She's staying downstairs now? "She lives downstairs. I love her dearly. She's 87 and I'm 90 and we're still going 61 years later," Duke laughs.

My grandmother used to say when you're old and your bed gets moved to the living room, the next move is to a box.

Kitty walks into the room looking frail, unsure on her feet and slim to the bone. Wearing her pajamas and slippers, she sits down in a chair alongside the Duke. I like Kitty a lot. She has been a champion for many social causes and is a remarkable person. Every time I've been in her presence, Kitty has been very sweet and engaging. The three of us always have a laugh or two. When A.I. creates the prototype New England aunt, she's it.

Kitty's father, the late Harry Ellis Dickson, was the associate conductor of the Boston Pops Orchestra for many years. In 1975, Dickson conducted the Boston Pops at the Inaugural Governor's Ceremony of his son-in-law, Michael Dukakis. Dickson was a big shot. Whenever legendary Pops' conductor Arthur Fiedler didn't come to work, Dickson would fill in.

One time, I told Kitty I had an Arthur Fiedler story. Oh, did she perk up quick. "Scott, tell me right now." Kitty said as she grabbed my arm. My Kitty-Dukakis-bonding moment. Here we go!

It was 1976 and my hometown of Methuen had just built a new state-of-the-art high school with a large theater hall. In celebration of the opening of the school and to christen the hall, they had the Boston Pops perform a concert. It was a huge event and everyone in the town was present. (The last big event in Methuen was the American Revolution.) I was ten years old at the time and went with my family. I was very excited to see the larger-than-life Boston Pops' conductor, Arthur Fiedler. But most of all, I wanted to see if I could get his baton as a souvenir.

Watching Fiedler conduct the orchestra on July 4th at the Esplanade was like watching Larry Bird play. You knew you were experiencing something special. Fiedler had wavy white hair and a white mustache. He looked like Albert Einstein with a weight issue.

The show was to start at 7:00 p.m. The audience was in their seats and the orchestra was in place. Everyone was excited to see the great maestro christen our town stage. There was just one small little issue. The main attraction, Fiedler, hadn't yet shown. Oh, no.

An hour went by and finally an announcement went out on the P.A. Fiedler was caught in traffic and would be arriving shortly. Two hours went by. Say hello to three hours. The patient crowd grew anxious and concerned. People were hoping and praying Fiedler hadn't been in an accident. It was the '70s, this was how we behaved back then.

Finally, at 10:34 p.m., here comes Fiedler driving into the parking lot, jumping a sidewalk and leaving the car there. I witnessed this because I had gone outside to wait for him. He stumbled out of the car, as shit faced as I've ever seen a human being since. As he made it to the entrance, I said to Fiedler, "Hi I'm Scott and I'm a big fan. Can I have your baton after the show?" Without hesitation or missing a stride, Fiedler responded, "Fuck off, kid," as his gifted and talented hands pushed my face away. Through my watering eyes, I watched him enter the school.

Kitty laughed. "This story doesn't surprise me the least bit. He was a terrible man, and our family used to have to socialize with him way too much of the time," said Kitty.

Harry Ellis Dickson once said in an interview. "I was probably as close to Arthur Fiedler as anybody ever got, and that wasn't very close."

Back in the living room, as always, Duke is smiling at Kitty like a smitten teenager. Nobody I've ever known adores his wife more than Duke does Kitty. Kitty has her head down as she sits with us. "I feel guilty. I feel guilty," she says. "You feel guilty because?" Duke asks. "I don't know what's the matter with me," she says in a sad voice. Duke smiles and says, "We're not getting any younger." "I don't know what my problem is," she says. "What was my problem when I was involved in that debate?" Duke suddenly asks her. "Why wasn't I all over that death penalty question? Kitty, I can't explain how that question was so obvious, that we didn't prepare for it." Kitty gets up from her seat, "I can't talk about this right now, anyhow," she says and leaves the room to go back to bed. Duke gives her a big smile as she exits stage left.

The more energized and agitated Duke laments, "Scott, I'm not quite sure why we didn't get that in detail in the debate preparation (and so forth). If I could have answered that question correctly, I could have become the president of the United States!"

Wow! How many people in the history of this country could legitimately have uttered that last sentence? Not many. These are the feelings I wanted to come out, if they did actually exist. I'm reminded of Marlon Brando's famous line in the 1954 movie, *On The Waterfront*, "You don't understand. I coulda had class. I coulda been a contender. I coulda been Somebody."

The Duke's post-political career has been quite successful. He's lived a comfortable life as a political science professor at Northeastern University in the falls and at UCLA in the springs. He's admired by millions of people across the country and the world.

But loss of any kind can torment you for the rest of your life. You watch a boxing match and sometimes, when a boxer's been hit by a big punch to the face, he smiles. He's hurt, but he wants to make his opponent feel that the pain is meager enough that he can just brush it off. I feel like the Duke has been that fighter, smiling for the last 35 years after experiencing a huge political, personal and public blow.

Before you ran for president, how well known do you think you were across the country? "So-so. Lots of places I wasn't particularly well-known." When you have been criticized in public life, especially when they get personal, do you ever get upset by it? "Sure, I did. But what's the point of being negative, Scott? What does it accomplish?" Have you ever called someone up or confronted someone who criticized you? "Yes. I don't recall it happening a lot though. But when people have been negative towards me, I was determined, if possible, to keep it on a positive road."

Governor, I read a statement that said your presidential campaign seemed to be mired in confusion during the general election. Do you think that observation was fair or unfair? "So much of this depended on the shape of the campaign and the emphasis we put on particular issues including the death penalty. If you don't do it, don't be surprised if it gets a little confused."

The polls said you had a big lead over Bush. Do you think the people in your campaign were in the mindset that it was already over and you all kind of froze the ball a little bit? "You mean to think it was already in the bag?" Yes, you said it happened when you lost to Ed King in your bid for reelection. "Nobody with any sense would have thought that at the beginning of a general presidential election campaign." Well, something went awry. "I think lots did."

Governor, it seems to me the Bush campaign brilliantly sold a bill of goods to the public during the presidential election—that whatever you said or did in the past or present was a negative— and a good portion of the American public bought it. "They did and I didn't counterpunch." You were keeping it positive and smiling. Duke nods his head. Did you feel like Bush was disrespectful towards you during the campaign and the two presidential debates? "No. Not like That Guy treated Biden."

"Scott, I have to be honest with you. I don't know of I've ever told anyone this. I was kind of bored during my debates with Bush." Is that right? "Yeah." Is that even legal? I can't stop laughing to myself. For all you political junkies who analyze every word and expression of a candidate during the debate, here you go. You want honesty? You can't handle honesty!

I try to go down the more difficult roads in small bits at each visit. We spend the remainder of the visit talking about the Red Sox. Despite the fact that they've finished in last place three of the last four years, this is our safe place. It's a relief to discuss other people's losses. Red Sox are always good for that.

Duke checking up on an ailing Kitty.

Stop Littering!

The Pledge of Allegiance of Greece: *I shall never bring disgrace to my city, nor shall I ever desert my comrades in the ranks; but I, both alone and with my comrades, shall fight for the ideas and sacred things of the city.*

I usually visit Duke at 2:00 p.m. His mail is typically dropped between the screen door and front door. He has a mailbox nailed to the front of the house, but it looks like it's from the 1800s and can't hold much more than a post-it note. I always arrive in time to hand Duke his mail and he always thanks me. I feel like I'm 88 years old doing it and one of these day's he's going to rub my head and say, "Nice job, Sonny."

You don't still pick up litter when you walk, do you? "I do. If I weren't hurting so much from that darn deck fall..." You know they're out there again fixing the deck. "I know. The town came along to look at it and turns out they didn't do it according to code, so now they have to rip it up and do it all over again."

No wonder those guys were staring at the deck with a look like, *Who forgot to give the envelope to the inspector?* The saga of the front porch deck continues.

You picked up litter from the public sidewalks for many years. "And will resume that as soon as I'm able to bend and so forth. But 90 is 90, you gotta watch it." Why do you do it? "I couldn't stand the mess. I'd be out walking around and there would be all this crap around," Duke says passionately.

"When we moved into the house in the 1960s, I saw all this crap and graffiti as well. So, I called the commissioner of Public Works, and I said, 'Hey, we gotta do something about this, it looks terrible.' He was a good guy, but he just didn't seem to think this was a problem. I told him it looks like hell! Can't we fix it? Anyway. Long story short, he didn't do anything about it."

I can't stop smiling while he's telling this story. If you've ever sat down with a grandparent for more than a few minutes, you appreciate these last two paragraphs. He has a burst of energy and is on a roll.

"Scott, I told you the story about getting stopped by the woman." Governor, tell me again. "Well, I finally said enough already, and I decided to go out and start painting over the graffiti." So, you bought a can of paint? "Two cans. One was green and one was blue. On a Sunday morning, I went out and started painting over the graffiti. About five minutes later, a woman stops and says, 'Oh, is this a committee clean-up thing or community improvement project or something?' I said, 'Yeah, you're looking at him!'"

I laugh. He tells this story with perfect comedic timing and female voice imitation. Classic. Governor Michael Dukakis will be appearing at Giggles this weekend for three sold-out shows!

"I was just out there by myself, and it's God-awful! In Brookline, the whole town is just covered with this stuff. Well, it's been a long time since." Did she help you that day? "No. She was just inquiring. Neither she, nor many other people as best as I could determine, seemed to be bothered by it! This is a beautiful town, what the hell! So that began my clean-up campaign." Duke is as animated as I have ever seen.

Duke is truly an American success story: A three-time governor and a man who almost became president of the United States and the leader of the free world who humbly began his public service career picking up garbage and painting over *Bobby loves Donna*.

"Finally, we got a new commissioner of Public Works who cared a lot more about graffiti than his predecessor, who didn't care at all it seems." So, they started cleaning up Brookline? "Yes, we've made real progress in Brookline, but what about my walks to Boston, who's going to take care of that? Nobody, obviously, because Boston wasn't cleaning it up!"

You started cleaning up Boston too? "As soon as I hit the Boston line, I started doing some stuff, yeah." If the Duke had been elected president, he might have personally made America clean again.

You've been doing this forever, even before you were governor? "Yes, in Brookline, this is my town. But at some point, when you become governor, you don't want to be out there still doing it." And post-governor? "Yes." Have you ever seen someone drop something on the ground and yelled at them for littering? "Occasionally I would see someone and I'd say, 'Who do you think's going to pick that up?'" I can't stop laughing

"Scott, they would look at me and, of course, at that time, I was usually pretty well recognized, and they would be kind of embarrassed and stuff. I'd tell them to just pick it up and throw it away. Usually they would do that." *Honey, I'm home and I just got scolded on the street by Governor Michael Dukakis for littering.*

Governor, I have a theory. "Scott, go ahead." My theory is that you like things very neat, orderly and organized, and you want everyone else to follow suit. "Yes, I want to live in a community that is attractive," Duke reiterates.

If the Keep America Beautiful Organization is looking to select a poster child for a marketing campaign, I know an older, sweet, Greek-American man I think would be a great fit.

Governor, despite your position, you were riding the subway each day to work. You were riding the public bus to appointments. You were shoveling the snow off your driveway. You cut your own lawn. "I always liked cutting the lawn," says Duke enthusiastically.

You didn't cash out. I can't imagine how much money you could have made off your success and name recognition. Nobody I have ever heard of in your position chose to live like, frankly, the rest of us. Except for you. Did you live life the way you wanted to? "Yeah, I did." Most people with your achievements "wouldn't do that," Duke finishes my sentence for me. "I don't know about anyone else. I cared about my community. I cared about my state." Did you try to live your life in a way that wasn't flashy? "Yeah, I mean that's not me." Were you comfortable in a room with people who were trying to make lots of money and rise up in the ranks as opposed to the average Joe?

"I think I was comfortable with most people. But by the time you get to where I got, they spent a lot more time talking to you than vice versa." They were interested in what you could do for them? "Not necessarily. At times, yeah."

"Scott, I had a position of major responsibility and carried it out as best I could. But I always had this very strong feeling of civic responsibility and that all of us have the responsibility to do things. As a citizen, I had a responsibility too."

Except for your family, this was your greatest passion, public service? "Yeah, for sure. And I would still be picking up litter, if I hadn't fallen through that damn porch."

If You Live Long Enough

Scott, Our granddaughter finally left us two weeks ago and she will be buried on Sunday. I'll be in touch next week. Mike.

Every time I leave the Duke's house, my last act is to scream upstairs to Kitty and wish her 'goodbye'. "Bye Scott," she always says in a sweet voice. In the three-plus years of my visits to the house, she's not been well, sometimes appearing better than others, but always in her pajamas or bathrobe.

I walked to Duke's house on a picture-perfect day and Kitty's home nurse answered the door. She led me into the living room where Kitty has been residing in a hospital bed. Kitty was balled up on the bed engulfed in blankets with barely enough energy to let out a faint groan to recognize my presence.

Duke was sitting in a wingback chair right next to Kitty holding her hand, *The Boston Globe* newspaper on his lap and *NY Times* beside his chair. He gives me a big smile and says, "Hello". I instantly thought maybe I should leave, but Duke was clearly happy to see me and he told me to sit down.

I'm not a doctor, but it's evident that Kitty is actively dying. Her face has a yellow cast. It's tough to see such a vibrant person slowly fading away. I've been present in the hospital for my father's death and my grandmother's. Those memories came rushing back.

My Grandma Rose died on the first day she had ever been in a hospital in her entire life. She waited for all of her grandchildren to fly in from their homes across the country to be at her bedside. She took roll call and died. As she flat-lined, one of my sisters began to cry and knocked over a Diet Coke can. As it crashed down, my grandmother awoke to see if everything was alright and then died again.

My beloved father, Norman Kerman, died in 2006 after being in the hospital for a week. The first five days, he engaged in animated conversation. One of the main topics of discussion was the on-going conflict between the Israelis and the Palestinians. Clearly not much has changed in the past two decades. The last two days of his life he was unconscious and his breathing continued to get more and more labored. When he took his last breath on earth, his six children were not only at his bedside, but on his bed. It's a surreal moment you never forget. It was the most emotional, exhausting and life-changing week of my life. When you meet your parents for the first time, you're meeting the world at the same time. Nobody remembers that. But you'll never forget seeing them for the last time.

Duke looks more fragile physically than I've seen him. Clearly, Kitty's decline in health has taken a noticeable toll on him. It's a lot to ask of a 90-year-old to be a caretaker for a loved one. The visiting nurses have come into the picture full-time recently. I'm glad they're here.

After an uncomfortable few minutes amongst an ailing Kitty, it was evident that we shouldn't talk in the living room. Duke suggests we move to our usual spot in the kitchen. Sounds good. I could tell that my visit would be a nice break for him. I was honored to be allowed in the house under the circumstances. Once we sit down at the kitchen table, we seamlessly continue the conversation as if we just came back from a lunch break. The kitchen feels like we're in our own bubble, away from all of life's problems. How's Kitty doing? "She's 87 years old, what can I tell you?" he says. Enough said.

Duke's living room is littered with framed pictures of his grand-children. He speaks about them as much as he does his children. He had shared with me some months ago that his granddaughter had brain cancer and that it wasn't looking good.

How are you doing with your granddaughter's loss? "What do you do when you know from the day she was born that she wasn't going to make it?" She was born with the condition? "Yes. This was not something that happened that surprised us." How old was she? "When she died, she was 22." He looks down on the ground and you could feel the weight of Kitty's illness and his granddaughter's recent death was too much to focus on.

"So, what do you think of the team?" Duke asks. We're both happy to change the subject. I know when he says 'the team' he means the Red Sox. What would people do without sports to take their attention away from everyday life problems? I talk about the latest goings-on with the Sox. Red Sox ownership is penny-pinching despite the fact that they have the highest ticket prices in Major League Baseball. "What's wrong with them?" Duke asks. I don't know. Seeing that the Duke personally knows the ownership group, maybe he can make a call and ask them.

When you were young, you liked the Boston Braves as much as the Red Sox. "Yes, I've always favored the underdog. In all of life." The underprivileged? "Yes, those folks. I felt like an underdog myself, mostly because my parents came to this country as immigrants and worked hard and did well."

Governor, tell me about your diet. You've been very healthy and very active when you're not falling through porches. Duke laughs. "When I was growing up as a kid, I ate a lot of Greek food, which I eat even now and like a lot. A Mediterranean diet. I never had any interest in liquor. I can't stand the stuff. I don't know why people drink and get pleasure out of this. But I never got any pleasure." You never drank at all? "No, I mean a cup of wine or something, but I didn't particularly like it. I would rather have tomato juice. Just never did, it was interesting."

Growing up my mother used to make us drink V8. It's disgusting. The only way I can compare the taste is if you drank your own vomit. It was just another way for parents in the '70s to cut corners with their kids. Why buy vegetables for our children when we can have them drink a medley of carrots, celery, beets, parsley, lettuce, watercress, and spinach juice? OK, I've just thrown up in my mouth writing that sentence.

"I couldn't understand why people like to drink alcohol." Any type of alcohol, champagne, beer? Not even for a toast or something? "Nope." So, the Dukakis home didn't have alcohol on the dinner table? "No, we had wine, but I didn't drink it." He starts laughing. On cue, Kitty makes a moaning noise from the other room. Kitty has been very public in the past about her battle with alcoholism and depression. Through Kitty's efforts, she has helped countless people realize they're not alone in this lifetime fight.

"You know what happened to my brother?" Duke blurts out of the blue. Yes, I do. I was meaning to revisit that story at some point. So, your older brother and only sibling, Stelian, is riding his bicycle on Winchester Street. He gets hit by a car and is left in a ditch to die. He spends four months in the hospital, never regains consciousness and dies. "Yes, it was just awful." You found out a year later who'd hit him and decided not to proceed any further? "Yes. Scott, what would you have done?"

In our conversations, I've always enjoyed when Duke has asked me my opinion or inquired about my life. He's doing this more frequently. This is a heavy question to answer. Clearly, he wants to talk about it.

Governor, I've thought a lot about this since we last broached the subject. I would have done exactly what you did and not attempted to pursue criminal charges. Without witnesses to the accident, it would have been very difficult to prove any fault of the driver. Duke nods.

Stelian's mental difficulties were bound to come up in any legal proceeding and… "What would have been the point," Duke says finishing my thought. "He's never coming back," Duke says with emotion as he tears up.

Did losing your only sibling at that age change your perspective on things? "I don't think it changed my perspective on things.

It was tragic. We were very close, he was gone and never woke up." Did you ever seek any counseling? "No. Scott, I was fortunate enough to have a family that, to a great extent, has given me the support I would have had if he was still alive. I have eight grandchildren and they're terrific. If I stay alive, I'll probably be a great grandfather."

A beautiful black Labrador, Pops, takes that moment to come bounding into the kitchen looking for love. My first reaction, while petting the dog, was to ask, You guys didn't get another dog, did you? "No, it's visiting." Duke's granddaughter Ali comes into the room and the three of us have a nice talk. Ali is an investigative reporter. She's Pops' owner. She gives her grandfather an all-consuming hug. It's a beautiful moment and it looks like the both of them needed it. Another point in the win column for family.

Ali and Pops head out for a walk. Pops will come back during my visit multiple times to check in and get some attention. Pops is the perfect dog to add levity to Kitty's ongoing health situation and the loss of their granddaughter. Pops is a true Dukakis, knowing how to read the room and serve the public with the attention and caring it needs. I'm very glad Ali and Pops are here.

Who's on First?

Dateline. April 7,1992. My life-long friend Robert and I decided to do a baseball trip and attend the Red Sox opening game of the season at Yankee Stadium. Yankees vs. Red Sox. It's rare that these bitter rivals played on opening day at Yankee Stadium. This had not happened since 1970 and was exciting stuff for a baseball fan.

I had attended a number of games at Yankee Stadium and I appreciated one of the true meccas of professional sports. The place dripped with nostalgia and greatness from the likes of Ruth, Gehrig, Mantle, Jackson and Jeter. Despite past abuse from Yankee fans, I've always worn my Red Sox hat in enemy territory. My father was buried with his Red Sox hat on, and I plan on doing the same.

The bleachers at the Old Yankee Stadium were full of deranged, drunken, disgusting lunatics. We figured, with it being opening day, maybe it wouldn't feel like a riot at a mental asylum. We were wrong. From the moment we sat down, we had everything thrown at us from peanuts to batteries. We were called every cuss name known to mankind. *It's bad enough you're bringing up my mother, but my grandmother, too?*

A forty-something guy who had broken free from his Yankees straight-jacket approached us in the third inning. He told us we wouldn't live past the seventh inning and his eyes refused to blink. After being doused with more food and half-consumed beers, we finally grew weary of sitting amongst the insane. We left at the bottom of the sixth inning, escaping our scheduled public execution just under the wire. The whole section stood up to celebrate our departure. In a last, final act of public humiliation, thousands of Yankee fans began pointing their fingers at us and chanting: *Dukakis! Dukakis! Dukakis!*

I walked onto Duke's front porch deck and survived. Feels like that needs to be on a car bumper-sticker next to: *I climbed Mount*

Washington sticker. I ring the doorbell and Duke answers. Both of us are clearly happy to see each other, even though I was at the house just five days ago.

We make our way to sit in the dining room. A new venue for today. On my way, I say 'hello' to Kitty who was lying awake in bed in the living room. She says something that I couldn't understand. I say, Kitty, It's good seeing you!

The visiting nurse had made herself at home and was curled up on the couch in the living room. She had her Air Pods in and acted like she was a Dukakis family member. Don't get up, the 90-year-old man who's hunched-over, limping and paying you will get the door. You go back to your playlist and rest your eyes.

"I'm still hobbling around. I should be walking normally by now. That fall on the porch deck didn't help," Duke says as he gets himself a drink of water and sits down. That front porch deck will forever be known as Lee Atwater.

The dining room has a big picture window and sun fills the room. You get nice sun in here. "Isn't it nice?" A radiator original to the house sits behind him. There's nothing like radiator heat. It can heat up a room in two seconds and is very comfortable. My house was built in 1920 and we removed our radiators to install central air. I was more upset when those radiators went than when my Aunt Linda died.

"What street do you live on?" Duke asks. Mason Terrace. Governor, do you know anybody on Mason Terrace? "I knew everybody on Mason Terrace." We both laugh. I'm sure you did. "I had some good supporters there," Duke smiles. Duke sounds like an old-time politician or an old-time salesman. I don't know if there's much of a difference.

Duke has been asking a lot about myself and my thoughts lately. I'm usually the one asking him questions. I'm honored when he does it. I don't have any friends like Duke, and he doesn't have any friends like me. But we sure get a kick out of being around each other.

Did you ever consider nominating Jesse Jackson as vice-president? "I don't think I really considered it." Jackson finished second to Dukakis in the primaries with 29 percent of the vote. What were your feelings about him? "Mixed. I certainly liked what he stood for at his best. He was an important guy. Jackson was a remarkable man in many ways, but he was difficult to deal with." You told me before he was a pain in the ass. "Did I?" Duke laughs. "He was, but I admired him."

"Is he still alive?" Duke asks. Wow, the *Alive or Dead* game. I'm pretty confident he's alive, but he could have died on a Sunday during a Patriot's game and it got by me. I quickly check, well within my ten-second limit. Yes, Jackson's alive and is 82 years old. "Still relatively young, I thought he was older." OK, Governor, that's very far from young. "Not from where I'm sitting." Touche.

You've told me a few times in the past that you couldn't understand how people could be dishonest. You said that you can't believe that people would not tell the truth—that you don't have a choice, but to tell the truth. Do you respect people who have been dishonest to you? Duke spits outs instantly, "No!"

Is being dishonest the number one reason someone would lose your respect? "It may be one of a number. But it's how you conduct yourself and whether you wield the authority you have in a way that meets high standards. It may not involve money; it may involve all kinds of stuff. I would never hire a person who had integrity problems, and people knew it. I kind of had an invisible firewall from the beginning."

"You know Scott, I got wonderful kids and grandkids, and I can't say enough good things about them. They're honest, and people of high integrity for which I'm very proud." Duke and Kitty have three children. Kara lives in San Francisco. Andrea lives in Colorado and John lives in Brookline.

Governor, I saw John last week in line in the CVS. I said 'hello' to him. He was picking up medicine for you. "John is such a terrific, terrific son and guy. He kind of keeps this place together these days."

During the second presidential debate, Duke revealed that he and Kitty had had another child who died about twenty minutes after birth. I decided not to ask him about this because I think we've discussed enough of his personal tragedies.

You ran the Boston Marathon. Was running important to you both physically and mentally? "Yeah." Did you enjoy the mental aspect of it? The clearing of your head? "Yes, for sure," Duke laughs. "Part of it is the Greek thing. Greeks are runners." Yes they are, Governor.

"I remember, I saw my first marathon when I was three. I started running shortly thereafter. I was running cross-country before I was even in cross-country. I was running competitively starting at eight or nine."

I'm pretty sure when we were young, we all ran in the woods or in a field and ran races with our friends. But, Duke articulates these same youthful experiences in ways that makes you think he was training for the Olympics.

"I became the catcher on the elementary school baseball team because nobody could catch a swinging strike." Duke loves saying this and gets such a kick out of it. I laugh every time. I'm a human laugh track. I enjoy being an adopted grandson, if only in my mind.

"I was a pretty good catcher, but there were two other catchers, Eddie Reddish and Bob O'Connor who were better than me in high school. Reddish lived in the Point. O'Connor lived two houses down from here." Did you stay on the baseball team? "No, I went out for the tennis team and ended up as the Captain." Are Reddish and O'Connor still alive? "I don't know. Probably not. If they are, then they're 90 years old. That's old." Good point.

Despite Duke's baseball career ending in high school, decades later his name would be chanted in the Yankee Stadium bleachers during a Yankees vs. Red Sox game just feet from Monument Park where all the great Yankees have plaques. A first for a Greek elementary school catcher. Fellas, make room for a plaque in the Park.

You Sure Have Grown

The Duke's doorbell is old-school. You ring it and it's as loud as the church bells for a Sunday service or a coronation. Duke has lived in the house for over 60 years and still gets startled when it goes off. To me it's a magic bell, because shortly after I press it, Duke appears from behind the door.

Governor, I have to show you a picture from 1977 when I first met you at an ice cream smorgasbord fundraiser in my family's backyard. When you look at yourself, what do you think? "I look damn good," Duke says with pride. Yes, you do. "I'm taller in this picture than I am in most of them." Yes, you are.

The reason he looks like Andre the Giant in the photo is because he's standing behind my seven-year old brother and alongside 11-year-old me. Many positive words have been used to describe Dukakis in the last 70-plus years of his adult life, but I'm confident *taller* was never one of them, until today.

Governor, you were very gracious that day. A few days later you phoned my house to thank my parents for having the event. I answered the phone. "How old were you?" I was 11. You and I had actually talked about the Red Sox at the event.

Back in the 1970s, if the phone rang at your house, it was a big deal. We had six kids in my family so I would run to the phone hoping to get to it first. If I was Greek and was first to the phone, well you know...

I answered and you asked to speak to one of my parents. I asked who was calling and you said "Michael Dukakis". Wow! I gave the phone to my father and, after a couple of minutes, you asked my father if "your son who answered the one I talked to about the Red Sox?" My father said, "most likely" and you asked to speak to me. What! Me? We talked about the Sox for a few minutes and then you had to go back to being the governor of Massachusetts. Governor, that few minutes made quite an impression on me—the idea that someone of your importance would take time out in your busy day to speak to me. Duke just listened and smiled.

Because of my interaction with Duke as an 11-year-old, I was never intimidated when talking to someone, no matter their title or standing. The definition of self-esteem is 'how we perceive and value ourselves' and it's developed during childhood. My small interaction with the Duke went a long way.

We're interrupted by the doorbell ringing. Clearly the nurse wasn't rattled by the noise, as she didn't even flinch. Duke gets up and answers the door. It's a strange, middle-aged guy who has come uninvited to the house. He wants to discuss with Dukakis his theory about the Isabella Gardner Museum art heist. This theft occurred in 1990, when 13 expensive works of art were stolen. The stolen art has been valued at hundreds of millions of dollars. Here we go, buckle up.

The conspiracy theorist at the door believes that George H.W. Bush, Queen Elizabeth, CIA, MI5 and the Pope were all part of the robbery. I don't know about that, but I used to tell a joke about them and a rabbi walking into a bar. "Can I come in to go over it?" Unsurprisingly, he has a manifesto that he hands to Dukakis.

It looks like it was bound 20 years ago. He asks multiple times if he can come in. That's my cue to stand up and go towards the door so he can see me.

Duke handles the situation like a true gentleman and tells the guy he's busy with a long interview. The guy departs with a promise to return at a better time. Perfect, let me check my schedule. How about never?

Though the message was very, very different, Duke can relate to the conspiracy theorist in one way. Duke has walked onto many porches uninvited. He's rung thousands of doorbells in his life to spread his message to the community that he represented or looked to represent.

Were you a good fundraiser? "I never had a money problem, but that's partly because I think I didn't spend a lot of money." Duke is infamous for admittedly being frugal. I can relate. I can't check out at a store without asking if there are any coupons I'm missing? Any employee discount? How about a friends and family discount? I feel like we're friends. Am I the millionth customer? Anything?

"I put heavy emphasis on grass roots, door-to-door, and personal contact. That's the way I ran these campaigns." If Duke had unlimited time to campaign for president, he would have preferred to have rung every doorbell in America. That's a lot of porch decks to possibly fall through.

Governor, what is it like being well-known and having so many strangers know your name? "As you grow up in this business, more and more people know you. You meet a lot of people at the same time. It happened gradually." When you speak to strangers and you say your name, do you assume that they will know who you are? "It depends on where I am. If I'm in the Greater Boston area, quite often. A lot of people respond to my name, or they'll say 'Dukakis, that's a familiar name. Are you related to the guy?' I'll say, 'Yeah, I'm the guy.' They'll say 'Oh, my God.' Duke belly-laughs.

Do you enjoy the attention? "It's fine. I don't crave it. It comes with the territory." You've been famous in the Greater Boston area since the early '70s and globally since 1988. "It's a long time to be famous," says Duke as leans back in his chair and laughs.

What kind of music do you enjoy? "A mix of stuff. You know, I was a musician of sorts." Is that right? "Played a good trumpet in my youth. Loved doing that. From way back, I was in elementary school playing the trumpet. People said I was very good at it." With that sentence, he sounds like every grandfather in the history of our country.

"I like jazz, I like popular stuff." Do you listen to music currently? "Not too much." If you were to listen to music, would you use a record player? "Yes, of course. What else is there?" Duke laughs at that obvious question. Well, actually...

Do you watch movies? "Not so much these days." Did you back in the day? "From time to time, I wasn't a movie freak." (I would have bet good money that if the word *freak* came up in our conversation it would have been about Trump.) Do you have any favorite television shows you enjoy watching right now? "I still prefer daily news." News is your entertainment? "That and reading." You lived a life where you were always out and about going places, didn't you? "Yes, but if I was home in the evenings, I was more likely to be reading something interesting rather than turning on the television set."

I'm so relieved! I don't have to ask that uncomfortable question if he has a television. I don't see one on the first floor of the house. I was a bit worried he hadn't made the transition from a radio to a television. Not a given.

Do you still drive? "No. I decided to stop at age 87." Do you take Ubers and Taxis to get around? "I like to get on the T if I still can." You still go on the T? "Yes, from time to time. Not as much as I used to." You know that's pretty incredible. Not many 90-year-olds are riding the T. "That's the way I live. You'd be amazed at the number of people who see me on the T and say, 'you probably don't remember this, but I was on the T with you in 1970 something or 2014 or whatever and so forth.'" He chuckles. "Riding the subway gave me the best position to connect with the folks I was supposed to be representing. I don't think Charlie Baker was ever on the T." As Duke throws out a haymaker, somewhere, Baker's ears start ringing.

Baker, the former governor, would be referred to as *that guy* if the position wasn't already filled. "Which is one of the reasons the T absolutely collapsed," Duke continues. Baker didn't run for re-election for governor as more information leaked out about what a mess the MBTA system had become under his leadership. He took a cushy job as president of the NCAA.

Do you have a cell phone? "No, I don't anymore." Duke may be one of the few people in the country over nine years old who doesn't have a cell phone. I understand the whole old-school way of living, but even people who go off the grid aren't giving up their cell phones. What happened to your cell phone? "I think it got lost." Lost or stolen? I know of a number of individuals and groups that may have stolen some expensive art who could have taken it. Where did that manifesto go?

Hometown Hero

I'm a walker. I walk everywhere. I walk to the grocery store, pharmacy, appointments, etc. I live two miles from Fenway Park and have walked there each morning for the last 20 years. I touch a Fenway brick, say a prayer and walk home. It's a blessing. Brookline is a walking town. In all my years living in Brookline, I've knocked into Duke many times during my walks.

If you hang out on the street with Duke for more than a minute, people will come over to speak to him. Usually with such reverence. He loves every second of being the Pope of Brookline.

Governor, you've lived in Brookline your whole life. Have you ever thought about living anywhere else? "No, we've been very happy here." What does Brookline mean to you? "I've always loved this town. It has its issues and stuff, but it's a good community."

If you had become president and served two terms in Washington, D.C., do you think, at 90 years old, you would still be living in this house? "Yeah, what's the matter with the house?" Duke snaps back. I laugh. Governor, there's nothing wrong with it. It's a wonderful house. For a public servant. We both laugh. He's getting my humor now. A year ago, I would have never let that line fly. "It's a beautiful house." Yes, it is, Governor, it's awesome.

You've walked these same streets for 90 years. "That's right." Does walking in certain spots in Brookline spur on memories for you? "Yes, to the extent that my memory is intact. I'm clearly not remembering things I used to remember fairly easily."

They say with old age, people may not remember what they had for lunch but can vividly recall things from as young as four years old. Duke's voice gets loud and enthusiastic. "Scott, what can I tell you? I do remember certain things, like for example, when I was five

115

years old. I remember where I was when we were about to have the hurricane of 1938."

I'm thinking how that sounds so long ago. I wonder if that was the same hurricane where a certain young woman from Kansas, Dorothy Gale, was filmed suffering a concussion and having one crazy-ass dream.

"I was playing on the street with some pals. I remember walking down Brighton Road, which is now Route 9, getting home and going to sleep." Were you scared about the impending hurricane? "Never gave it a thought. Don't remember other things that happened in those days, but I do remember that storm and waking up the next morning seeing huge trees that had been uprooted up and down Route 9. Incredible sight." He makes catastrophic events sound almost appealing. I can tell Duke has put himself back there in his mind. With the recent death of his granddaughter and Kitty's failing health, I think losing himself in a simpler time was just what the doctor ordered.

Well, since we're on the subject of natural disasters, it was 46 years ago yesterday that the Blizzard of '78 hit Massachusetts. You were famous for wearing sweaters during those press conferences and on television. "I still wear sweaters," he chuckles. Do managing the state's response to the emergency?

"I just remember going to sleep, waking up the following morning, getting out of bed and looking out. I don't know how many large trees were completely uprooted. I don't remember other things that happened at the age of five." Duke is back reminiscing about the hurricane. I've noticed in the last few visits more than ever, he's been having difficulty transitioning from one topic to another.

What has changed is that he's now comfortable saying, "I don't remember," as opposed to attempting to struggle with his memory. Six months ago, he would have eaten his right arm before admitting to any chink in the armor.

But, do you remember much about being the governor during the blizzard of '78? "Yes, but less than I do about that hurricane of 1938," he says in such a way it makes me laugh. It made such an impression on you? "Oh my God, you have no idea. These huge trees just uprooted," Duke motions with his arms. "I slept right through the hurricane." Duke chuckles to himself.

"Scott, did I ever tell you that we bought a six-family house consisting of six units with nine rooms each? I turned it into the second condominium building in the history of Brookline." He's back with his Duke-isms. "I sold those units for $13,500 apiece and used the profits from that sale to buy this house mortgage-free. We've lived here ever since. Pretty good investment."

The Duke and I are kindred spirits when it comes to our homes. I grew up in a time where people tightened their spending belts to pare down their mortgage and paid it off as soon as possible. Growing up, I remember if someone we knew had lost his job, my father would say, "If he has his house paid off, they'll be just fine." This resonates with me to this day. One of the proudest moments of my life was making the last payment of my mortgage.

"Scott, I was doing some interesting reading on the period we're talking about now." So, the eighties? "Yes." Duke loves to read political books about that decade. "You never had a feeling that H.W. Bush, in particular, wasn't somebody who didn't have a fundamental integrity to him and to what he was doing. I didn't agree with his policies, but…"

Dukakis just went out of his way to compliment the guy who played dirty politics to keep him from becoming the leader of the free world. He's like the divorced guy who keeps going on and on about his cheating, ex-wife's chicken cacciatore.

Where would you put Ronald Reagan on the integrity scale? "Not my style. Not my whatever. He was a guy who was pretty traditional for when it came to what was going on. But we've never had anything like we're seeing with *that man,* and it continues, it continues! " If you're scoring at home. That man=That guy=Donald Trump.

"How many times do you have to be indicted before someone says: 'Enough already, send him away!' And they're using every trick in the book to try and keep him from having to go to trial."

Trump is never far from Duke's negative thoughts. Feels like history is going to treat modern republican presidents much better than they deserve in comparison to Trump. I have a cousin who hates Trump so much that you could be talking about the weather, and he'll say *what really is inclement is that horrible Trump.*

"Now, maybe I did go overboard. But remember, Scott, I had come up from the ranks in Massachusetts. This state today in terms of its integrity and its quality of leadership is like night and day to what I grew up with politically." Governor, corruption was just rampant back in the day, right? "I don't know if it was rampant, but there was a lot of it. I learned even more about how bad it was when I got into politics." But that didn't discourage you? "No. One of the things I wanted very much to do was to help clean up the state from a corruption standpoint, and it was pretty bad."

A young Michael Dukakis had a lot of confidence that he could accomplish things, would you agree? "I don't know if I had a lot of confidence, I just knew that's what I wanted to do. Turned out it took awhile; it could be changed, and we changed it."

It must be pressure-packed and obviously very intense being governor? "No, I didn't feel a lot of tension. But that's, in part, because I didn't have any problems as governor," Duke laughs. Governor, are you sure about that? Any? I couldn't help but think how my father, in his later years, used to say that his six kids never, ever gave him a stitch of trouble. Exactly. We were perfect angels. Sometimes memory loss isn't such a bad thing.

Better To Have Loved and Lost?

The Duke answers the door with a huge smile and greeting. We will visit in the dining room again, as it's more private than the kitchen these days. The visiting nurse for Kitty needs access to the kitchen so she can get her snacks. The nurse is still lying in the same spot she was when I left ten days ago. She might be the most rested person in the greater Boston area.

As usual, Duke's house is an oven. The only thing that keeps me from passing out on this day is the opened crack of the window, which allows in a nice breeze. This reminds me to never take ventilation for granted. Duke sits there cool as a cucumber in his flannel shirt and button- down sweater. "Hey Scott, I know you probably don't agree, but I'm getting a chill. Could you shut that window?" Huh? Sure, Governor. I'm just going to write, *Help Me,* on the window before I sit back down.

Governor, if I had a crystal ball and told you on the day before you were going to announce your run for president that you would lose, would you still have run? "Probably not. You don't run to lose. You run to win, and it looked very promising at the time. Sometimes things work out okay, sometimes they don't. It just didn't work out as it should have."

Do you appreciate that you had 42 million people vote for you? "I know, but the other guy had 48 or something." It was an improvement from the last two presidential elections for Democrats. Jimmy Carter in 1980 and Walter Mondale in 1984 lost by greater margins.

Do you feel like you paved the way for Bill Clinton to win in 1992? "You never know, Scott, what influences people's votes—why they vote for you or not for you. Every election is different. Maybe it helped."

Were you handicapped in a way because Carter's and Mondale's elections had gone really poorly? You're asking a lot of people to switch their votes to a different party. Wouldn't that seem to make it more difficult to win? "No. Remember I started that race after the convention 17 points ahead and yet lost. Who can claim that?" Unfortunately, no one else. No plaque for that title.

When we first began this project, Dukakis was very dismissive of the 17-point lead after the Democratic Convention. As we've progressed, he has seemed to work it through and is taking more ownership in losing such a big lead, or maybe he's just become more comfortable with voicing it.

Do you think the Willie Horton political ad during the general election was dirty politics? It's been described as vile and racist. "I think it was unfair and inaccurate on many levels. Every state had a furlough program, including California, when Reagan was governor."

Horton was a black man and a convicted murderer. Horton raped a white woman and stabbed her partner while furloughed under a Massachusetts' program put in place while Dukakis was governor.

The TV ad is considered by many, the most racially divisive ad in modern political history. It highlights the Horton incident and says that Dukakis 'not only opposes the death penalty, but he allowed first-degree murderers to have weekend passes from prison.' The ad was meant to portray Dukakis as soft on crime, and it was very effective. The Willie Horton ad was produced by campaign manager Lee Atwater.

I channel game show host Monty Hall, from *Let's Make A Deal*, with my next question. Governor, there are three curtains, and you have to pick, in order, which incident hurt you the most in the presidential campaign, post-convention: The Shaw debate death penalty question; the Tank photo; or the Willie Horton political ad.

"I think the debate question is first, Willie Horton second, and to this day I really don't understand the issue over the tank picture."

Let's talk about Lee Atwater. He was Bush's campaign manager in 1988 and a hired political thug. "He was a decent guy, he was okay." So, you have no ill will toward Lee Atwater? "No." Not even a little bit? "Not at all."

Duke's words are genuine. He chooses forgiveness every time. He carries no anger or bitterness toward anyone who may have treated him unjustly in his life. We all could learn a life lesson from him to let bygones be bygones.

I read that apparently Atwater, on his deathbed, called you on the phone to apologize for his role in the way he handled the campaign. Do you remember that? "I remember you mentioning it to me." Atwater called it the 'naked cruelty' of the 1988 campaign. He died shortly after the election in March, 1991. "Sadly, how old was he?" He was 40. Is it any consolation that someone so deeply involved in how the Bush campaign handled themselves, felt bad about his actions in his last days on Earth? "It's an election. Lots of stuff happens that we wish we could do differently."

I know you don't like hypotheticals, but play the game with me one time. "OK." If we make a trade and Atwater's running your presidential campaign and your staff is running Bush's campaign… Duke finishes my thought. "Do I win?" I nod. "Possibly, yes."

Let's go over the famous tank picture. During the presidential campaign you go to a tank factory to support a buildup in conventional weapons, like tanks. Your staff decides that taking a photo of you driving around in a tank, while wearing a helmet that was too large, was a good photo opportunity. "In retrospect, it wasn't a good idea." You think?

What did you think about the criticism of the tank picture? "I really never took it that seriously." Do people mention that picture to you still? "These days not as much." I think it was unfair the way they portrayed you. "I don't think it was unfair." So, nothing is unfair in politics? "Well, sometimes things are unfair, but you'd better expect to be photographed in a variety of conditions." Not by your own people, Governor.

Unfortunately, there are a lot of people who only know of Dukakis from that picture. I've seen it used as a meme on social media more times than I can count. Good grief. If Trump had done the same photo, his cult would have compared him to General Douglas MacArthur.

Duke was accustomed to fun photo ops during his political career. He took a picture in October, 1986 with the current Boston Celtics stars, Larry Bird, Robert Parrish and Kevin McHale at Hellenic College in Brookline, where the Celtics practiced for many years. He's wearing an official Boston Celtics warm-up suit and is standing on a folding chair holding a basketball. Placing him at the same height as the Celtics stars. McHale is holding a basketball on top of Duke's head, and there are big smiles all around.

When I showed Duke the picture, he smiled. Governor, four legends standing there. "No, just three. This was always one of my favorite photos." You were showing the lighter side of Michael Dukakis? "I guess so." Had Larry Bird been alongside you in the tank photo, you might have been president. Duke laughs. "That would have been a better idea."

I just want to mention that you do talk hypothetically. In 2008, in an interview with Katie Couric, you said, 'Look, I owe the American people an apology. If I had beaten the old man (Bush, Sr.) you'd never have heard of the kid (Bush, Jr.) and we wouldn't be in this mess. So, it's all my fault and I feel that very, very strongly.' "I said that?" Yes. "Well, that's right, I should have beaten him."

Governor, what advice would you give young people who are going out to start their careers? Obviously, you worked closely with students as a professor of political science at Northeastern and UCLA. "Getting deeply and actively involved in public life is one of the best things you can do. It's not the only thing you can do, but one of the best things you can do. I've never regretted for one minute the opportunity I've had to do good things and make life better for people."

How about the people who say, 'If I go into public life, I'm not going to make a lot of money'? Duke pauses for a while. "You won't make a lot of money." We both laugh. "That doesn't mean you can't do a great job and have a great life, but you're not going to be a millionaire. Plan to live modestly, but you don't have to wear sack cloth and ashes." I had not heard that reference in 50 years. "But get your kicks from being deeply and actively involved in what's going on. If you want to make a lot of money, don't go into politics."

You didn't go into anything for the money? "No, that's for sure." You never got lured in by the big money, did you? Duke shakes his head. Had you worked as a lawyer for all these years you'd be much wealthier. "Yeah, I guess so." It wouldn't have been as fulfilling? "Not at all. Not interested."

"I meet young people all the time and they're very proud of their country and doing great stuff, especially immigrant kids. They're doctors, lawyers, engineers. How well they've done. It's amazing!"

"Scott, have I told you my haircutting story while attending Swarthmore College?" Tell me again. "I go to Swarthmore and the relatively few black kids at Swarthmore can't get their hair cut. So I say 'screw it', I can cut hair; come to me and I can cut your hair. So I gave them their haircuts. I'll be God-damned if I they have to try and to find a black-only barber."

"At that time, black kids couldn't get their hair cut at a regular barber shop. Jesus, can you imagine in Philadelphia, Pennsylvania." That was a big deal back then. "Sure was." Did you catch flak? "No, thankfully, it was Swarthmore. It was a liberal school. A haircut!"

Duke has the enthusiasm of an eight year old. He's so genuinely happy to have contributed to the betterment of mankind and to see people succeed. Another great lesson for all of us.

You graduated from Harvard Law School in 1960. Did you like law school because of the critical thinking aspect? "No, not really." Did you like law school? "So-so," Duke makes a face like he ate some bad clams. What part of law school did you not like? "The law," he answers, with perfect comedic timing, I might add. We might have to take this show on the road at some point.

Governor, why? "I wasn't interested in the law; I was interested in public policy. But in those days, you went to law school because there was no public policy major." In the Harvard Law School List of Notable Alumni, the correction will need to be made. *Governor Michael Dukakis 1960 (But to be honest with you, he didn't really like it).*

Speaking of law, what are your thoughts on the Constitution? "I'm not sure I agree with everything in our Constitution. It's a document that has evolved over time. We're getting decisions from the Supreme Court that I've not been happy with and one of them is lifting the limits on campaign contributions." Yeah, Citizens United, they did that a while ago. "How long ago?" It was 2010, as I find out in nine seconds flat. Here we go!

Citizen United v. Federal Election Commission: The Supreme Court ruling reversed century-old campaign finance-restrictions. It enabled corporations, outside groups and rich donors to spend unlimited funds on elections, thereby potentially and essentially buying the result. Governor, that decision changed the whole political landscape, didn't it? "Terrible decision. Jimmy Carter called it the worse decision the Supreme Court ever made."

Were you comfortable fundraising? "Yes, but we had rules, and we followed them. Makes it easy right?" Now there are no rules. I guess that makes it even easier. "Unfortunately, for all of us."

It was time to wrap up my visit for the day. As I was leaving, I walked by the living room to say 'goodbye' to Kitty. Kitty was laying on her back, her mouth locked wide-open, her face as white as a ghost and stiff as a board. She was eerily silent.

Oh shit, it looked like rigor mortis had set in. I've seen that look before with my grandmother and father. Did Kitty just freaking die? I look at the nurse and she's sound asleep, but most definitely still alive. Kitty, I'm not so sure of. I envision the first line in Kitty's obituary:

Kitty Dukakis, the former first lady of Massachusetts, died yesterday with Scott Kerman at her side.

I start looking around the room in blind panic. What am I going to do? Thankfully, the person who saved Massachusetts from ruin comes around the corner to save me and let me out of my predicament and the house. I give Duke a big hug 'goodbye' and he opens the door. As I walk out, the sounds of coughing blessedly ring out from the living room. Kitty's alive. I can mentally remove my name from of any rough draft of her obituary.

Plaque of name change that no one knows about.

Governor Dukakis official portrait
at the Mass. State House.

Currently Playing

I arrive a little earlier than usual for today's visit and carry in *The Boston Globe* and *NY Times* from the porch. I hand it to Duke and his reaction is as if I just handed him a box of Greek pastries. Unlike pastries, he'll find some contents in the newspapers very distasteful. It doesn't stop him from digging in with a smile on his face.

Duke keeps up on current affairs like no other. We spend a portion of each visit discussing the news of the day. If I'm not up on my current events, Professor Duke looks at me like I need to start filling out an add/drop form. I thought I'd spend this visit getting his opinions on important matters across the globe.

Governor, Russia invaded Ukraine in February 2022. Now, close to three years later, should Biden have tried to broker a deal with Russia and Putin and Ukraine and Zelensky?

"Scott, I don't know why Putin ever invaded Ukraine. Ukrainians are good people; they're independent-minded. What's the point of this?" Well, I think that was the issue. Putin thinks an independent, democratic Ukraine is a threat to him and Russia. "He's a nut!" Yep.

How would President Michael Dukakis have handled the current situation in Ukraine? "I would have tried everything I could to possibly bring the two leaders together in a way that would result in a peaceful settlement." It's probably best not to call Putin a *nut* when getting together. Just a thought.

Your view on the Israeli/Palestinian situation? "People are getting killed! Netanyahu has not been one of my favorite people." Is he a thug? "No, he's not a thug. He's a graduate of MIT and Harvard. You would think he'd be the kind of guy who would be able to do this and do it successfully. Netanyahu is in terrible political shape, and he should be. Enough is enough! Right now, the world needs peace and we are not getting it because of Putin and Netanyahu. I believe the Middle East situation could, and would, have been resolved years ago, if Netanyahu hadn't been there."

Have you ever met Netanyahu? "Yes, he and I were at MIT at a conference once. We sat next to each other." What did you think of him? "Seemed to be a decent enough guy." Was he smart? "I don't know, given what he's been doing lately, I wouldn't call that smart."

Do you think he's corrupt? "He's been under indictment for a long time." Does he remind you of Trump? "No, No. No. That's going too far." We both laugh. "Trump is really a thug. A bum," Duke moans. I'm impressed that he was able to say Trump's name. I think Duke made the exception for emphasis.

"How can I put it about that guy (Trump)? There's nothing normal about him. There isn't much that one could admire about him in public life. He's a grandson of German immigrants. He said immigrants are vermin, animals. He's disgusting!"

For a person who believes public service is one of the most important issues of your life, do you believe in mandatory national service? "I don't think so. But, if the country is in trouble, and it needs help from folks, including young folks, then I would support it. I don't think we need it now."

Governor, I have a friend who currently has two grown kids living at home. They're driving him bat-shit. He's leading the charge for mandatory national service so he can get the kids out of the house. Duke laughs.

What's your feeling about the police? "We should be proud of the police and not defunding them. I don't know what defunding means." Governor, I think the people who propose that don't know what the definition of defund is either. Do they think the police are going to work for free? "They're not thinking. We need well-trained, well-financed and well-supported police. The police need to act in a way that's compassionate, responsible and sensitive. They need to treat people well. But to get rid of the police, that's crazy."

Republican governors such as Greg Abbott from Texas and Ron Desantis from Florida are trying to expand their powers in defiance of the federal government by passing strict state immigration laws. What do you think of that?

"I think they have every right to do that." You do? I didn't expect that response. "To make governors an important part in the governing of the country, sure. Governors are more important than ever, especially concerning the immigration problem we're facing." Duke would have his liberal Democrat membership placed under further review for these last few responses.

You are 90 years old. The country will be 248 years old on July 4th. You have been alive for over 36 percent of the country's existence. "I never heard it put that way." We both laugh. What is your perception of the Republican Party during your lifetime? "There was a time when the Republican Party had an interesting group of people. Some of them were moderates who were pretty responsible. That has changed very dramatically and in a troubling way over the last few years with *that man*. Now, there are only a few moderate Republicans."

Can you believe that Trump will be the Republican nominee for president for three election cycles? "I can believe it because the Republicans are all over the place and disorganized. They don't have strong leadership, and the ones they have are pretty bad."

Was abortion a hot topic when you were running for president in 1988? "I don't think so." Roe v. Wade had been decided 15 years earlier in 1973. You didn't mention it in your DNC speech. It's one of the top issues in the 2024 campaign. "I know it was an issue for some people." How times have changed.

Are you happy with Biden's term as president? An animated Duke appears. "I've always liked Biden very much and he's done a remarkable job in the first term given all the moaning and groaning of the country. Scott, think about what we were going through with Covid, and he comes out the other side. He's emerged with remarkable strength and done a hell of a job under very difficult circumstances. I don't understand the pessimism of the American people with the Biden administration. We've come out of a period which could have been disastrous for us economically and come out of it in good shape."

Do you think you could have governed Massachusetts at President Biden's current age of 81? "Yeah, I think so." Could you have been president of the United States at that age, knowing what the job would take from you, mentally and physically? "That's a good question. I'm not sure I would try." Reagan was 77 when he finished his second term in office. "Reagan seemed very old during the second term; that's for sure."

What are your thoughts on Vice-President Kamala Harris? "I like her more and more. I thinks she's done a pretty darn good job being the number-two person. I think she's grown pretty significantly over the past few years."

Changing topics, Governor. Boston's never going to connect North and South Stations are they? "We better. This is the most ridiculous thing I've even seen." How' does it get done? "You build it." Would the federal government have to get involved? "I think that would probably be the case." Why didn't you do it when you were governor? "I had more important issues. It wasn't hot at the time." Why has it become so important to you? "Because it's a missing link in the city and metropolitan area. It's only five miles."

Every once in a while I'll see a mention of it in my news feed and I'll think of you. Duke laughs. You're not going to let it go? "No, I'm not going to let it go." Dukakis will haunt elected officials from the grave until the North and South Stations are connected.

Governor, does it bother you that people don't believe a lot of what the mainstream media is saying? "There's always been a lot of skepticism on both sides concerning the media. Too much misinformation is being put out there for lots of people to see. There are fewer and fewer newspapers across the country that carry influence. It's not going to get any better, I'm afraid."

Will newspapers be around in ten years? "I hope so, I depend on them." You would be 100 years old. "Well, my mother lived close to 100."

Governor, this means I'll be visiting you every week for the next decade. Once you reach 100, you're on your own. Duke smiles. Also, you need to start stocking some of my favorite snacks and drinks. He laughs, "Scott, happy to do it."

Queen For A Day

The Duke has a Massachusetts accent. When he says the word, *matter*, it comes out *matta*. I had a Massachusetts accent growing up, but if I wanted to pursue stand-up comedy and an acting career, I needed to learn to pronounce words correctly so people outside of New England could understand me. There's no sign language for how we New Englanders speak, but maybe there should be.

My accent is detected in words like *idea*. I say *i-dear,* which, if you really think about it, is the way it should be spelled and pronounced. Or maybe not, it was just an *idear.*

It's a 90-degree day and I walk into a hotter than usual Dukakis house. Duke is wearing a flannel shirt. He looks like he's melting in front of my eyes. Governor, it's a little hot in here. "I'm fine. Nowadays, it takes a lot for me to be hot." Ok, good to hear. I'm thinking maybe in an hour, I'll ask Kitty's visiting nurse if she can run an IV of fluids for me.

Governor, how did Kitty's mental health issues affect you over the years? "In a serious way. I love this woman dearly and she went through a period where…" Duke pauses for 30 seconds. "Scott, how do I describe it? Depression isn't a pleasant thing. It's very serious and needless to say, for a while, it was so frustrating. This lovely, bright, interesting woman would periodically go into these slumps and there didn't seem to be anyway out of it. We had tried this and that and nothing worked. Until we found something called Electrical Convulsive Therapy. ECT. I never heard of it. Shock! We met a wonderful doctor, Charlie Welch." Welch is considered a pioneer in the use of ECT.

"The profession was beginning to explore ECT and Welch talked about it with us, and I said let's give it a try. It was remarkable." How long did it take to see progress? "She had four or five treatments, and I have my wife back! The speed with which it worked was incredible. It was the damnedest thing I've ever seen. Kitty was back! Can you imagine? A different, different woman. It was just a shot of electricity. You figure it out."

"Scott, if you have friends or know folks who are suffering from depression, let me know because I want to help." I will. That's very kind of you, thank you.

The two people closest to Duke in his life, Kitty and his brother Stelian, both suffered from mental illness. Millions of adults and children are affected by mental illness each year in the U.S. I can only imagine how a Dukakis presidency might have addressed the growing mental health crisis leading into the 21st century. I'm betting it might have dramatically lessened the epidemic we currently face.

Governor, you hosted Queen Elizabeth in 1976, which was the first trip to the United States by a British monarch, and you were her first stop. I remember it was a big deal, right? "Oh yeah. It's a funny story. It was part of the Bicentennial celebration. We're all sitting there waiting—Mayor White, his wife Katherine, Kitty and me. All of a sudden there she was! Queen Elizabeth at the deck rail. I think she had come from Canada. Her royal yacht was parked in the Charlestown Navy Yard."

"She looks amazing. Lots of applause. She begins to come down the gang plank and begins sliding down." Duke makes a funny noise to imitate her sliding. "Kevin and Katherine are ahead of me and then it's Kitty and me. She comes down with a bump and stays on her feet." She does? "Yes, says 'good morning' or 'good afternoon' whatever it was." Doesn't skip a beat? "Nope. Quite an entrance." Were you ready to try to catch Queen Elizabeth? "We were instructed by the Queen's security to make sure to never touch her. But I wasn't going to let her fall, I don't care what anyone said," Duke joked. "She stayed on her feet and greeted everybody." Do you remember any conversation with her? "Just pleasantries. A very special day."

Governor, do you like compliments? "I prefer a compliment to an attack. Other than that, eh." Are you comfortable with people saying nice things about you? "I think so. But I am more interested in listening to their thoughts." Like when they named South Station after you? Duke makes a mocking face. We both ,laugh.

In your speech at the renaming ceremony, you said nobody was going to remember this. Anyone else would be beside themselves with excitement. The pinnacle of their life. My name is going to be forever immortalized in one of the main transportation hubs in the City of Boston. Not you. "Scott, I'm not a testimonial guy. If I'm still going strong and if I'm making any sense at all, I much prefer to be listening and not listening to praise for me, but listening to stuff that's helpful, interesting, valuable and constructive." That's wonderfully put.

How do you want to be remembered by the public? "I don't think I've ever been asked this question. I think the best thing about life is that one can make real contributions in ways which not only help to improve the world around you, but at the same time make it possible for you to make contributions that are important. To that extent, and I include Kitty, in this, I hope we've made some important contributions."

"Scott, you don't always achieve what you would like to achieve ideally. In my case, by and large, I think I've done that with the possible exception of the presidency, where I wasn't successful. But, to have a good and decent family, kids that you respect and admire, and to be successful in ways that make contributions to your society—I mean that on the whole—I think I've been able to do with few misses."

Is there anything left you want to accomplish? "As long as I'm still on my feet and taking nourishment, I hope I'll be able to contribute in some fashion for some time. Kitty and I have had a special life, and we're fortunate."

Do you follow the whole artificial intelligence wave that seems to be coming into our world at a rapid pace? "I do. But, at this point in my life, it's more trouble than it's worth." In 1933, when Dukakis was born, the discussions were about prohibition being repealed, making alcohol legal in the U.S., and Hitler coming into power in Germany.

It's been argued that A.I. will take away a lot of jobs. In your lifetime, you've watched many factory jobs disappear, along with the communities they had supported for generations. As an elected official, talk to me about the fear that your constituency had concerning losing their jobs to technology?

"That's always been the argument about new technology. We've managed, especially post-World War II, to absorb, create and expand, when people say it's going to take jobs. It brings other jobs with them. We've always managed to overcome it. We will do it again with A.I. Education plays a key role in having people keep up."

What was your favorite subject in school. "History, and it is to this day." Was there a teacher that made a lasting impact? "Yes, Grace Lamb, my fourth-grade teacher. Very special person. She had an impact." As Duke's memory fades, he has forgotten many names of important people in his life, but he hasn't forgotten his favorite teacher, Grace Lamb. This speaks volumes about how important teachers are in the fabric of our lives. My fourth-grade teacher, Mister Tardiff, was also my favorite teacher. Fourth grade is the best grade ever! I mean evah!

Can You Read Morse Code?

A hot and humid August day in Boston seems unfair. The locals suffer through seven months of winter to make it to the summer and some good weather. Can't we get a break, here? A few years back, Duke was scheduled to appear on The Grandstanders on such a day and Kitty was to accompany him.

The station manager called me to say that the elevator was broken and we would have to take the stairs up four floors to the studio. I left a phone message on Duke's pre-civil war answering machine. If he or Kitty didn't think they could climb the stairs in the oppressive heat, we could reschedule.

My wife, Adrienne, and I walked up the stairs with co-host Uncle Joe McLaughlin. It was over 100 degrees in the dark and oppressive stairway. When we finally reached the summit, each of us was sweating and panting.

We all agreed, there's no way two octogenarians were going to make it up the stairs. They're going to die, and I'll be to blame. I killed the Dukakis'. I turn and, suddenly, from behind the green-screen curtains, burst Duke and Kitty with big smiles,! Both are fresh as daisies and prom ready! "You made it," I exclaim. Duke shakes my hand and says, "Kitty and I are just relieved that all you folks made it up the stairs in one piece." Everyone laughs.

Governor, how important is religion to a community? "I think religion is an important force. I'm concerned about what's going on these days, because we have a guy who's running for president who professes to be religious but isn't at all." In what religion were you brought up, Governor? "Greek Orthodox and married a Jewish girl. Who wasn't entirely Jewish." Her father, Harry Ellis was Jewish? "Yes, but not practicing. Kitty was mixed religion. Kitty's mother didn't talk about it much, but she was something other than Jewish." After 60 years of marriage that was never cleared up?

"No." I can relate as my father was a non-practicing Jew and my mother was Armenian, but I was brought up Episcopalian, if you can believe it. "Why Episcopalian?" Duke asks. Well, the Armenian Orthodox church services are so painfully long that if parishioners actually die during the service, they will pause to bury the person and then continue on with the service as if nothing happened. Duke laughs. My parents had six kids, and my Armenian grandmother decided we can't do this to them every Sunday. So, each week, she went 'religion-shopping' to a different religious service to check them all out. She picked Episcopalian because the services were short and they had fresh donuts and coffee upstairs. Duke nods in understanding.

In my experience, a person's faith can be ever-changing and tested often within their lifetime. On May 23, 2008, I was diagnosed with Leukemia. There were a few hours on that day at the hospital when it wasn't clear what type of Leukemia I had. It was Memorial Day weekend and the oncologist on call was nowhere to be found. Based on my experience, I would suggest never going to the hospital on a holiday weekend if you can help it. You could end up having the security guard examining you and the cleaning staff reviewing your chart.

While I was waiting for the guy in the white coat to arrive, there was discussion between me and the residents where they concluded my situation was fatal. Thanks, guys, for the positive thoughts, you morons! In those fateful hours, I had to come to grips with the possibility of leaving my wonderful wife and beautiful eight-year-old twin boys forever. Is this really freaking happening? My faith was my only consolation. I figured I would be in heaven with God and get to see my father again. That's all I had left to cling onto.

Thankfully, the oncologist on call finished playing golf and came into the treatment room long enough to tell me I had a rare form of Leukemia called CML. In the last few years before my diagnosis, CML had gone from being a fatal disease to a chronic disease with the discovery of a new treatment. "Scott, take this chemotherapy pill once a day for the rest of your life and have fun watching your boys grow up," the doctor told me. I walked outside and the sun was setting. I looked up at the sky and all I could say—then and now—is, Thank You, God!

World War I ended 15 years before you were born. When your family gathered at the kitchen table, was the war brought up as topic of conversation? "Well, we were in the middle of a Depression and much of the talk was how World War I caused it." This paragraph is sponsored by *Let me tell you when things were much worse*!

Do you remember being fearful living in Brookline, that the fight in World War II would come to the mainland? "We certainly knew it was possible. It was constantly in my thoughts as a youngster. Yeah, for sure." You were six when World War II started. Did you have a bomb shelter at your house? "We didn't, but there were ones around around the neighborhood. When the sirens went off, we knew where to go."

"Scott, we shouldn't romanticize the past. Prior to 1950, this country was very different. It was intolerant and reactionary. Those were not good times and anybody who tells you that we need to go back to the 'good old days' to feel good about it, doesn't know what they're talking about."

Your father was a doctor? "Yes, he was a general practitioner and OBGYN." He was a baby doctor? "Yes. He served mostly an ethnic clientele. I remember he had his own office at 454 Huntington Avenue in Boston. He was beloved by his patients and worked hard for 52 years." Do people still come up to you and say your father delivered them? "Not as much now, but they did a lot over the years."

What's your definition of socialized medicine? "I don't know what the hell that means. We have it now, it's called Obamacare. It's the closest we got to it, thanks to a guy named...?" Dukakis prompts me, he's in professor mode. Was it Ted Kennedy? "No, it wasn't Kennedy. Do you remember the guy who put up his finger and voted 'Yes?'" John McCain. "Right, yeah, by one vote, and it was a Republican. One vote! So people could have healthcare!" Duke yells"People have always raised hell about it. When I think about the uproar about socialized medicine when I was a kid, we're close. The Republicans are still fighting it. A lot of people do have government-financed medical care. But there are still folks out there who don't have the security of knowing if they get sick, they're going to be treated."

"Scott, not to change the subject, but because of our conversations, I've thought deeply about how I should have answered the death penalty debate question." OK, go ahead. This is new ground. I sit up even straighter, as he brings himself back to that moment in the debate.

"Look there's nobody in this world that I love more than Kitty. We've had a remarkable relationship over many years, and I love her more each day." Silence. Continued silence.

Governor, that's beautiful. Perfect. You nailed it! Everyone knew where you stood on the death penalty. Duke interrupts me. "Much better than the lousy answer I gave. Here we are," Duke takes a deep breath and exhales. This was a big moment. It's as if he just found the key to open a door that's been locked since 1988; like he just got an elephant off his back. Pun intended.

With our visit over for the day, I hug Duke. I'm a big hugger. If I like you and I see you, get ready, I'm hugging you. Duke is not a big hugger, but he's warmed to my hugs over the years. We've settled on the 'goodbye' hug only. I walk out the door and head to the post office to buy stamps, just in case people ask me how to contact the Duke.

Theory or Hypothesis?

The Dukakis' have lived in their home for 60 years and have never locked their front door. I never knew this, as with anyone who has not tried to burglarized a home. I've always rung the doorbell and waited for Duke to answer the door.

Governor, your granddaughter told me you don't lock your front door. Why's that? "Scott, if our kids come over, I want them to be able to get in the house." Don't they have keys? "Yes." I know you had an open-door policy as governor, but I don't think it should include your home. Governor, that's not safe. How about we start a new initiative and lock the front door moving forward. "Sounds like a good idea." My visit today has already been a success.

I've noticed Duke's memory is starting to fade at a more rapid pace. He'll struggle to remember things past and present that he recited seamlessly a few months ago. He'll apologize for not recalling something and I'll remind him that it's not a test. No worries. I decided to spend ten minutes of each of visit reading to him parts of his Wikipedia page. A little refresher on a life well-lived.

Governor, I was looking at your Wikipedia page. It says you were described at times, both when you were governor and running for president, as having a *reserved and stoic nature*. "Me?" Yes, you, Michael Dukakis. "I hope not." Duke sounds like he was just accused by his mother of eating a cookie before dinner. Don't shoot the messenger. I would not describe you in this way, and I've known you quite awhile. Do you think, at points of your political career, this was a fair observation? "No. How can a Greek be stoic?" Have you heard that description of you before? "No. Never." It's not terrible. "But it's not me. I'm not stoic."

Governor, I just looked it up. The word *stoicism* is Greek. It's a philosophy that offered the Greeks a framework on which to build resilience, well-being, peace of mind, and moral character. It's all good! You're the poster child for stoic! Duke gives me a look like he should have locked me out.

John F. Kennedy was born on Beal street in Brookline. Robert Kennedy was born on Abbotsford Road, Brookline. You have said JFK was your favorite president in your lifetime. "Yes. We never had anyone quite like him. When he died, I was absolutely crushed." You met him, right? "Yes, we're both Brookline boys." Where were you when you heard he had been shot? "I was coming out of my law office and someone said, 'Kennedy had been shot!' We lost a great man, no question. His assassination was a very powerful thing. Some guy comes along and puts a bullet in his head. This is the United States of America. Ugh. God." Did you cry when it happened? "I'm quite sure I did."

"First, I was just shell-shocked. Here is this extraordinary guy, who is relatively young, and he's gone. Just gone! It was awful. It was just awful! He reflected on so much of the kinds of things that I believed in. It was terrible. Just terrible." Duke gets teary-eyed.

Duke is more emotional today than I've ever seen him during my visits. I think Kitty's deteriorating condition has taken a toll, which is a quite natural. His partner of over 60 years is at the end of her life, and this man of great competence and ability can't do a thing about it.

Was Kennedy a big influence in your strong belief of public service? "Yeah. Look, it happened. So the rest of us had to go to work and try to redeem his memory and carry forth on what he and others like him believed in. The country continues and it always does." Duke starts getting emotional again. "That day, some jerk from Texas comes along and puts a bullet in his head," he shouts. Kitty's visiting nurse enters the kitchen to get something. She hears *bullet to the head* and beelines it out of the there. She can get her cottage cheese when calmer heads prevail.

Do you have any JFK theories? "I've read a couple of books on theories of what might have taken place. The guy was alive and well and doing great stuff, then he's dead. I just...God!" Duke lets out a sigh. "If you think things are bad now, there's nothing that compared to that. How the hell did that guy get close enough to put a bullet in his head?" I'm pretty sure if the visiting nurse heard that, she's booking it out the door and never coming back. Just two friends talking about JFK's assassination on a Tuesday afternoon. Unlike watching Duke's DNC speech, it feels like we're not the only guys in the world who would be having that conversation at that moment.

Time to switch gears. I think picking Senator Lloyd Bentsen of Texas for your vice-presidential nominee pick was a good choice. "So did I." You picked a highly respected, prominent political figure in Bentsen. I think it said a lot about the confidence in yourself that you chose someone of great stature.

"I was a strong believer in having a running mate who was a strong, capable person. Not because I thought I would be shot." Oh geez, not again. We've said the word 'shot' more times today in this kitchen than at a vaccination clinic. Is the nurse even here anymore? I'm worried I'm going to end up being the one administering Kitty her meds.

Does the VP nominee move the dial either way for an election? "I think so. I think people are very interested in whom you pick." Do you think people will change their vote based on the VP selection? "They could. I think some people will." Enough to sway the election? "It's possible."

Governor, do you consider living 90 years an achievement? "I never thought about it in that way. I guess in some ways. Scott, do you think it is?" I do, absolutely, especially when you look at the narrative of somebody's life. The average life expectancy of a male in the U.S. is 73 years. Governor, you were able to avoid getting hit by a moving train. "Good point and I rode a lot of them!" You sure did. "Scott, I'm not what I was when I was 80." You're doing pretty good, my friend. "Yeah, I'm hanging in there."

So, for $19.99 on eBay, you can buy a photo of you with actors Howie Mandel and Stephen Furst of *St. Elsewhere* from the 1984 episode where you made a cameo appearance as yourself. (St. Elsewhere was a fictional hospital located in Boston.) That was a great show. "Scott, has anyone bought it?" I'm sure you have plenty of Dukakis groupies who probably have it hanging up somewhere. If only this was the most famous photo Duke ever took.

In the photo, Dukakis is in a running suit while Furst puts a stethoscope to his heart, giving him a quick check-up. I remember the episode. The storyline was that Dukakis hurt his ankle jogging and went to the emergency room at St. Elsewhere. The doctors didn't believe he was really Governor Dukakis. Riveting stuff. A tearjerker where you needed a box of tissues nearby. Duke looks at the photo carefully. Do you remember this? "I remember Howie Mandel. I look good in this picture. I had a running suit just like that one." It's probably yours. Most likely somewhere in this house. "Possibly." Depression babies don't throw out clothing.

As a professor, were you considered an easy or hard grader? "I don't think I was easy. But my students seemed to respond to leadership in the classroom and that's what I tried to do." So, you were a hard? Like, you're in Dukakis' class and you need to bring your A game or you're getting a C? Duke laughs. "You better ask them. I think I was fair."

I'm pretty sure I know the answer to these questions, but have you ever had a Facebook account? "Facebook account?" Duke looks at me like I just asked him if he's ever been affiliated with the Communist party. How about Twitter? Duke answers "No" in a barely audible voice. Let me finish this intense line of questioning. Have you ever had any social media account? He just looks at me. You've never had any of that? "No reason for it." You still have a computer? "I do, but it's off and on, mostly off."

On that note, it's time to leave for the day. I walk out to an impending thunderstorm, as I look at my phone and make my return to the 21st century.

Who Plays Duke in the Movie?

At the end of my last visit, I had this conversation with the Duke: "Scott, I'm going to an event next Thursday at Northeastern." (Duke taught political science at Northeastern University for 20 years.) Great, what's it for? "Me." Duke points his finger at his chest. I'm so amused by him, I can't tell you. Is it a retirement event? "I don't know what the hell it is. People wanted to do it, finally I said okay. About 150 people. I'm not going to be thrilled about it. They're showing up at Northeastern at 1:30."

Is it Michael Dukakis Appreciation Day? "I guess. I mean, I wasn't happy about it. People kept saying you got to do this, okay, alright, alright." Are you going to speak? "I guess they expect me to say something like, thank you. But that's not my thing." Well, you spoke on some of the biggest public stages for decades. But I get it. I'm sure you'll have a great time. "Ahh."

The day after the event, it was covered on the front page of The Boston Globe. Duke still has lot of cachet in this town. As we sit down for our next visit, I'm excited to discuss it with him. Governor, how did the event go? "Well, I resisted it strongly. The kids wanted to do it, so I finally said okay and it turned out to be kind of a nice afternoon event." I'm sure it was. What was the theme? "The theme was Mike Dukakis, I don't know."

You acted as if you would rather go the dentist. Duke shrugs his shoulders. Who was there of note? "They brought back former governors and current Governor Maura Healey was there." Northeastern did a nice job. Did you speak? "Very briefly. I resisted it." Dukakis has been in the public eye for six decades and relished it. He now appears to dread it. It's tough to be shy and introverted and hold political office. The only time a politician says "no comment" is when they were just indicted or were caught sleeping around on their wives. Well, except for that guy.

Northeastern is special to you. "Yeah, It is. What progress Northeastern has made over the years! Wow. Even since I was a kid. It has become a very impressive institution don't you think?" Absolutely. "It was a good experience for me. I loved teaching there. It's a strong academic and research community. I was there in a teaching role for 20 years and it was a very important part of my existence."

At the event, your son, John, read a letter from former President Bill Clinton in honor of the celebration. "John did a great job speaking." I'll read Clinton's letter to you. "Okay."

Clinton wrote:

"I'm proud to join the many distinguished guests gathered today at Northeastern University celebrating your remarkable lifetime of public service. From affordable housing and health care to improvements in public transportation and the creation of hundreds of thousands of good jobs, you prove that smart government really can make a difference, a positive difference, in people's lives. Our nation is better off because of your example. And your impact will only continue to expand as your students continue to grow, lead, and succeed."

"I appreciate the kind words. We were very close, and I like him a lot."

I also pulled the text of some of the dignitaries' remarks about you from Northeastern's website. Let me read them to you:

Former Republican Governor William Weld said in his remarks:

"If I had to summarize in one word what the legacy of Mike Dukakis is in politics and the United States, that one word is honesty. He was an inspiration to me now and was for his whole career through the presidential race."

Governor, a Republican politician saying something positive about a Democrat politician. Take note, as this may be the last time this ever happens. "Weld's a good guy."

Former Governor Deval Patrick said:

"It was you who taught him the word: 'grassroots campaign'. You told him that frankly it is about the power of showing up, and talking to people, and listening to people."

Patrick also said you were an "example of stewardship, integrity, and honesty and that you set a positive tone in the Commonwealth and beyond." He "recalled getting untold numbers of phone calls from you about trash that needed to be picked up." So, you called Governor Patrick about litter? "Maybe." Who else can contact a current governor of Massachusetts directly to report Dunkin coffee cups scattered over Beacon Street?

Current Massachusetts Governor Maura Healey said:

"Mike Dukakis has devoted so much of his life's work to looking after those who are vulnerable. He continues to build and create a legacy. Dukakis has a legacy of building incredible teams; engaged, curious team-players who are all about advancing the public good. Not ego, not self-aggrandizement. The legacy of Mike Dukakis is one that we all have to live up to day in and day out."

You're a big fan of Governor Healey. "Absolutely. She's doing a great job!" She's obviously a fan of you, too. "It's nice to hear."

Northeastern University President Joseph E. Aoun said:

"I've never seen an impact such as yours. You've inspired young people, and you still inspire them. You open doors for them. You made them realize that public service is a noble goal,"

Wow, what an event. Governor, you're the only person I know, who was lucky enough to attend his own funeral. Duke laughs.

You've been a great mentor to so many of your students. I've seen it during my visits; the many phone calls you receive from former students looking for guidance. "That's part of the thrill of teaching, being able to reach out to young people and have an impact on their lives."

Do you understand how many people you've touched in your life, not only as a political leader, but on a personal basis? Do you appreciate that? "Oh yeah. Very much. I hope they appreciate it." They do. I do.

Do you know how extraordinary you were as a political leader to be as compassionate, respectful and engaged towards people from all walks of life? "I didn't think it was extraordinary, but okay." I want you to know that is was, and is. "Good to know."

Duke seems a little tired today. I'm betting the event took it out of him. I usually stay two hours, but today I wrap it up after an hour. As always, he walks me to the door.

It was great seeing you, Governor, that was fun. "Scott, call me Mike from now on." Okay. I give him a big hug. I love you, Mike. "I love you, too." I'll see you next week. "I look forward to it, Scott." Me too, Mike. "Scott, stay close." I will.

The End.

Scott continues to visit Mike regularly.

www.ingramcontent.com/pod-product-compliance
Lightning Source LLC
Chambersburg PA
CBHW072217100925
32436CB00023B/545